SALLY J. MCKIRGAN

THE
GIFT
OF
THE
GREAT
RAYS

Inner Peace Essays

A Course In Miracles and its Promise of Freedom

BALBOA.PRESS

A DIVISION OF HAY HOUSE

Balboa Press books may be ordered through booksellers or by contacting:

Balboa Press
A Division of Hay House
1663 Liberty Drive
Bloomington, IN 47403
www.balboapress.com
844-682-1282

Interior Image Credit: Sally J. McKirgan

Print information available on the last page.

ISBN: 979-8-7652-3131-9 (sc)
ISBN: 979-8-7652-3132-6 (e)

Balboa Press rev. date: 08/09/2022

A COURSE IN MIRACLES
– ANNOTATIONS

T = Text (T-13.VII.9.1)

13 = Chapter

VII = Section VII (of Chapter 13)

9 = Paragraph 9 (in Section VII)

1 = Line 1 (of Paragraph 9)

Preface: Preface by page number

W = Workbook (W-pl.159.5.4)

pI = part I of the Workbook (pII = part II of the Workbook)

169 = Lesson 169

5 = Paragraph 5

4 = Line 4 (of Paragraph 5)

M = Manual for Teachers (M-4.X.2.9)

4 = Section 4

X = Part X (of Section 4)

2 = Paragraph 2 (of Part X)

9 = Line 9 (of Paragraph 2)

in = introduction(s)

r = Review (workbook)

fl = Final Lessons (workbook)

C = Clarification of Terms (in the Manual for Teachers)

ep = Epilogues (end of Workbook and Clarification of Terms)

P = Psychotherapy: Purpose, Process and Practice

S = The Song of Prayer

DEDICATION TO GOD.....

"Father, it is Your peace that I would give, receiving it of You.
I am Your Son forever just as You created me, for the
Great Rays remain forever still and undisturbed within me.
I would reach to them in silence and in certainty,
for nowhere else can certainty be found.
Peace be to me, and peace to all the world.
In holiness were we created, and in holiness do we remain.
Your Son is like to You in perfect sinlessness.
And with this thought we gladly say "Amen."
A Course In Miracles W – p Il. 360: 1-7

.....AND TO YOU DEAR READER:

"Miracles come from God to His dear Son,
Whose other name is You.
Prepare yourself for Miracles today.
Today allow your Father's ancient pledge
to you and all your brothers to be kept."
A Course In Miracles W-pI. 106: 4-7

CONTENTS

A Course In Miracles – Annotations v

Dedication To God.. vii

Painting Watercolor Title: The Separation: Earth in the Balance xiv

Foreword by Bruce Rawles xv

Preface... xvii

Acknowledgements xxi

Introduction: Inner Peace Column History xxiii

Letter to the Editor Guest Commentary, Dec.24, 2008 xxv

Photo: Peace Banner – Peace Fence Banner Ashland Railroad
      Fence xxvii

COLUMNS 2020-21

Pigheadedness: Time for self-reflection 1

United vs Divided: The Spark of Understanding...3

Want to be happy?.. 7

Change thoughts of Aversion to Mercy...9

Poem: The Winds of War 11

The Spring 2020 Moon reminds us: "I am There" 13

Painting Watercolor Title The Seven Continents Loving
Mother Earth 16

The Peacemaker – Deganawidah and the Great Tree of Peace 17

Poem: Above the Mess..20

COLUMNS 2019

Good Politics is at The Service of Peace 23

The Antidote to Hate is not more Hate 27

Poem: Refuse to Hate...29

The Pain of Loneliness – The mindless Supreme Court in Our Head 31

COLUMNS 2018

Easter Peace: "All Are Welcome Here" 35

Photo: #HateHasNoBizHere, Common Roots Café & The
      Main Street Alliance...37

Poem: Red Bi-Plane: Steel Sea..38
Just Do It" and Ashland's World Peace Flame.............................39
Christmas 2018: Part I, "Why Christmas?".................................43
Painting Watercolor Title: Three World Religions Join in Peace........46
Christmas 2018: Part II, "Why Christmas".................................47
Poem: You Are Forgiven...49

COLUMNS 2017

Learn to Acknowledge Projections for Inner Peace 53
Photo "Mt. Shasta's Heart, Mt. Shasta, CA 56
Being: "I AM" Pure Consciousness 57
See Either Love or the Call for Love 61
Poem: You can't get away from us, Mom..................................63
Whenever You Make a Judgment. 65
Poem: Apologize America 67

COLUMNS 2016

International Peace Day: Take your Temperature 71
Our Halloween Identity: Goblin, Ghoul or Angel..........................73
Painting Watercolor Title: Fly Like an Eagle..............................76
Choosing Peace During the Political Season...............................77
A Holiday Gift: Quiet Your Holy Mind......................................79

COLUMNS 2015

Your Beautiful Beneficent Mind...83
Tired of Violence 85
The Answer is Forgiveness: Look; Wait and Judge Not 89
Native American World Peace and Prayer Day 93
Painting Watercolor Title: Native American's Dancing...................96
Poem: Honoring Black Elk, Lakota Medicine Man........................97
The Promise of Christmas..99

COLUMNS 2014

Surrendering to the Inevitable..103
Say It with Love 105
Painting Watercolor Title: HELP!!...107

Graduation Advice to My Kindergartener..109
Case Dismissed: There goes the judge!..111
Poem: A Scaredy Snake?...113

COLUMNS 2013

Celebrate Easter: Choose Peace..117
The Inner Peace Diploma..119
The Light of Forgiveness...121
Painting Watercolor Title: One Family, One Planet; One People......124
International Peace Day & Internal Peace Day 125
Love Does Not Judge...127
Poem: My Sweet Little One...129

COLUMNS 2012

What Kind of Day do you Want: Grievances or Freedom? 133
The Peace of the Father..135
Photo: "Courage" - Bench at West Point...138
The Gift of Addictions 139
Golden Key to Inner Peace..143
Political Peace—Disagree with Kindness 145

COLUMNS 2011

Everyone Is your Valentine!..149
Poem: My First Best Friend...151
Painting Watercolor Title: Take Jesus off the Cross 153
The Field of Non-Judgment...155
We Can Be Kind: September 11, 2011 159
Be Thankful Love is your DNA...161
Poem: You Are Loved 163

COLUMNS 2010

Exclude No One from Your Love...167
Are You Loved? Yes!...169
Painting Watercolor Title: Daffodil Love...171
Finding Happy Birthday Peace..173
To Have (or not have) Holiday Peace..175

COLUMNS 2009

Happy New Year: Forgive Everyone Everything.................................. 181
Valentine's Day: Why not Love Yourself?.. 183
Know Your True Identity: Who are you?.. 185
Don't Blame God!.. 187
Poem: Walking on Water.. 190
Painting Watercolor Title: Walking on Water.................................... 191

THE GIFT OF THE GREAT RAYS

The Gift of the Great Rays.. 195
Poem: The Gift of the Great Rays.. 198
Painting Watercolor Title: Angel Star 199
The Promise of the Great Rays 201
About: A Course In Miracles..203

Afterword 205
Resources & Recommendations and Readings....................................207
References..209
Bio – Sally J. (Hammer Wensky) McKirgan...211

Painting Watercolor Sally McKirgan Title:
The Separation: Earth in Balance

FOREWORD BY BRUCE RAWLES

Being a lifelong truth seeker, Sally McKirgan is a devoted explorer, avid practitioner and effective communicator of Inner Peace; one feels that in her presence. For several years, when I lived in southern Oregon, I attended the enlightening study groups that she facilitates in person and now attend online. I enjoy her insightful writing and generous sharing of what is truly helpful. Like so many others, I treasure her friendship which we've all learned together isn't contingent on any specifics that can change. Our minds are capable of the true stability of inner peace – indeed the greatest gift! I appreciate Sally's friendly, egalitarian approach to everyone and her grasp of important ideas such as this: "This is the ego's world; the ego is part of our split mind. The trouble is we think it is the boss of us, our identity, and we believe it's telling the truth. It is not who or what you and I are, thankfully." I whole-heartedly recommend this book by Sally McKirgan.

– Bruce Rawles, ACIMblog.com editor and author of "The Geometry Code: Universal Symbolic Mirrors of Natural Laws Within Us; Friendly Reminders of Inclusion to Forgive the Dreamer of Separation," Youtube presentations with A School For A Course In Miracles and interviews with A Course In Miracles teachers and students.

PREFACE

"Can you imagine what it means to have no cares, no worries, no anxieties, but merely to be perfectly calm and quiet all the time? Yet that is what time is for; to learn just that and nothing more." A Course In Miracles T -15.I.1:1

Why the search for inner peace? The experiences in life with its challenges, joy and especially pain forms us, prompting the guidance of our inner spirit to seek peace. Some take up drugs, alcohol or addictive behaviors to find solace. As I considered what drove me to search for inner peace, it opened more memories than I bargained for. As I began writing, more and more details emerged, and this was becoming a memoir. The nagging questions of my life were: Why? Why me? What am I doing here, and what or who am I? I am happy to say I now know the answers, and I'll share them in the essays and poetry of this book.

I entered this world where the Olympic Mountains admire their reflection in Puget Sound and where Chief Seattle and his people fished, hunted and roamed in the tall forests. My Norwegian mother married a handsome Austrian who turned out to be a wife beater like his father and probably his father before him. She divorced him when I was a year old, but my infant ears would have overheard the violence maybe even seen it. After she left him, he kidnapped me, but the sheriff promptly rescued me a few days later. She said she saved me from growing up being beaten by an alcoholic. Thanks Mom!

I felt deprived for not having a father like Ozzie Nelson. Weren't all fathers like Ozzie? My mother remarried several times and I ended up having four fathers; well, the first one and then three step fathers followed. I won't go into evaluating them because like all of us they had their good and not so good qualities. But I did feel like a fatherless child. I gradually learned from several girl friends that there is no such thing as a perfect father, because after all they are human. They do their best. Some are quick to anger and some are not.

Another instrumental childhood experience came from church. I liked the Sunday school teacher, a lovely young woman who showed us a book with all the beautiful children of the world in their ethnic clothing. I was astounded by the wondrous exotic varieties of children and ethnicities in the world. I had known only people like my family, but these kids were amazing. The teacher said emphatically that Jesus loved them all. Really? Wow! I decided Jesus was OK! A few Sundays later we had to stay for the adult service. The fat red-faced angry preacher sermonized himself into a tirade telling us we were all sinners, we were going to go to hell, and that God was very angry with us. I turned my head and looked out the church windows at the peaceful swaying trees and thought, "I don't think so." Where did that thought come from, and why do I remember it? I chose to believe the Sunday school teacher instead of the preacher. I still do.

Our experiences form us like soft clay in the sculptor's hands or his chisel on stone as he chips away, eventually developing the psyche that becomes us, you and I. We grow up molded and formed by love, kindness, neglect, harshness, and more. I experienced the usual gamut life offers: feeling like a fatherless child; poverty; domestic violence; threat of the A Bomb; polio scare; and small-town closed-mindedness, like most everyone in the 1950's. We deal with the world's disasters and heartbreaks differently, but most of us feel like victims and want to blame someone. It is pain however that ultimately propels the search for the antidote. I knew at the core of my being there had to be an answer somewhere because really..."Is this all there is?"

I luckily found and married a wonderful guy and while raising our boys in Oakland, CA, I explored transcendental meditation, Hinduism, Buddhism, Muktananda, Rajneesh; I read Krishnamurti, Ram Dass, Gurdjeiff, Jane Roberts, Edgar Cayce, and other spiritual and mystical books seeking the solace I knew must exist somewhere. I stayed away from the Christian traditions of my early childhood, deciding that if there was a God, he was not very good by allowing pain and suffering in the world. Many of our friends joined the Est encounter groups, but we were drawn to an organization called the Creative Initiative Foundation, which Stanford professor, Dr. Harry Rathbun, had developed along with his wife Amelia. The focus of the organization was four fold: 1.) political work on the nuclear threat to the planet; 2.) a oneness, equality and inclusiveness of all religions and cultures; 3.) inner work examining prejudices, belief's and conditioning and 4.) a enlightened understanding of Jesus and God void of Christian dogma. My husband and I flourished in the community and attended spiritual retreats in the California Santa Cruz Mountains. The retreats helped us deepen and we opened up to others, re-awakening the mystery of God and Jesus. I had a profound mystical experience at the second retreat. Our involvement lasted for several years until the organization changed and eventually became Beyond War. After our involvement ended, I was despondent and longed for the community I had found. And since Jesus and God had been re-introduced into our lives, I searched for an enlightened Church, but not the standard doctrine.

I finally found the path that would lead me to the realization of the "imagine" statement at the beginning of this preface. I saw an article on the front page of the Sunday San Francisco Examiner in the spring of 1987. The headline: "A Marin County Group studies mysterious esoteric book." What was it? I had been reading esoteric books for years. I devoured the article. The next day I bought the book, A Course In Miracles, opened it, and immediately found a study group at the Walnut Creek Unity Church. It has been my companion ever since. And yes, that "imagine" statement is possible. It is a life journey and you get hints and glimpses of that statement and you know the promise is real and there's no turning back. Hooked like a fish!

Looking back I can see that my early experiences led me exactly to where I was to be. So instead of blaming the past, I now appreciate the journey. I understand who and what I am and what the world can and cannot offer. This is the ego's world and always will be. We are taught to buy into it and believe it has something to offer. When we find our gifts and figure out how to survive, then we can begin to search for the light the world excludes and the eternal Self, Spirit that is our inheritance. We are our own saviors; we are innocent, loved and not fatherless and we are welcome home any time, door's open…like right now! God is Love and so are you! You will discover this for your Self if you haven't because that is God's promise.

Sally Jean McKirgan

ACKNOWLEDGEMENTS

In loving appreciation to everyone whose life has intertwined with mine. You have all been my teachers. To my loving husband Carl, sons, Scott and Shawn, daughter in-law Mitsuko Jean, Grandchildren Luke and Kelsey, my brother Virgil, sister, Teresa and their families and to all my friends in Oregon, Washington, California, Colorado, Ohio, Georgia, and Florida; the Rogue Valley Peace Choir, Peace House, my women's support group, the Friday Course In Miracles study group and all Course friends I have met over the years; you will Always be in my heart.

Thank you to Ashland Tidings publisher, staff and editors Myles Murphy, Kathy Noah, Bert Etling and Justin Umberson for their help with the column from January 2009 to October 2021.

To all the wonderful 60 to 70 inner peace columnists who for 12 years contributed articles to the Tidings and continue to do so. Bless you peacemakers.

To Bruce Rawles, the first contributor to the column, A Course In Miracles teacher, writer, a spiritual friend whose effervescence is contagious with puns, wisdom and the wit to carry us out of the dream; thank you for the Foreword!

To Richard Carey, a great editor who edited these columns and now facilitates the Ashland.news Inner Peace Column. Richard lives in Ashland, he studies the Zen of idleness and scribbles out the occasional poem.

To Bert Etling, former Tidings editor and founder publisher of Ashland. News, for his gracious endorsement and continuing to carry the column; my deep appreciation.

I am ever grateful to the Cosmic Mystery, our elder brother, Jesus whose Mind gifted 'A Course In Miracles' to you, me, and the world with his message of forgiveness and the promise of inner peace; and to his scribe Dr. Helen Schucman who for seven years, 1965 to 1973 with the help of Dr. Bill Thetford of the NY Presbyterian Medical Center brought the Course into the world. To my spiritual teacher, Dr. Kenneth Wapnick, of the Foundation for A Course In Miracles, and all the beautiful souls who helped bring the Course forth into the illusion, I am forever grateful. The Inner Peace Column and this book of essays would never have been written, if not for the Course. God Bless you all as we travel to the Home We Never Left.

INTRODUCTION: INNER PEACE COLUMN HISTORY

As many students do, I kept a journal over the 30 plus years study of the Course and found that writing was helpful in my understanding and comprehension. In December of 2008 George Bush was President and being a peace activist I had had my problems (judgments) about him. What I wrote helped me, so feeling it might help others; I sent a letter to the editor of the Ashland Tidings. After all, it was Christmas, who couldn't use some peace? I didn't hear anything back, but when I picked up the newspaper on Christmas Eve morning, "what to my wondering eyes did appear" but my letter published as a guest commentary. It was a surprise and a gift! Make no mistake, I don't claim to be a great writer, I just love to do it.

A week later I stopped by the office to thank the editor and picked up an extra copy. As we visited I brought up the idea of more articles revolving around the idea of inner peace not just by me, but also include the many gifted spiritual teachers and seekers in Ashland. Ashland is quite unique in that way. The editor at the time was Myles Murphy and he was open to it. We discussed the logistics, resulting in my volunteering to facilitate the column, writing articles and finding others to participate. All paths, ideas, challenges and successes would be welcome. Everyone would be invited to submit articles because we both felt that inner peace was not exclusive to any one particular path, but to everyone, faith or non-faith. I was new to Ashland, but I was sure I could find people willing to contribute to a column on inner peace. I was very excited.

The column was to be a judgment-free zone. The paper put out the call for writers to submit articles and I began to compile and organize. The first column was by my friend, Bruce Rawles, published on January 31, 2009, "The Law of Cause and Effect."

The column appeared in the Ashland Tidings every week for 13 years until October 2021 when the Tidings ceased to be published by the owner of the Mail Tribune, Rosebud Media. Those 13 years saw nearly 500 articles from the minds and hearts of the wonderful writers who willingly shared their wisdom, wit and knowledge about their inner peace journey.

When Richard Carey began to write articles I asked to meet with him because his email moniker indicated he was an editor. That turned out to be true as he had been an editor for Microsoft for years and was the author of several books including one on poetry 'Prayers of an Infidel" and his talent was apparent. I needed an editor to help me compile this collection of essays into book form. I was also contemplating moving to Olympia and I needed someone to take over the column. He agreed to both then two things happened in October; first the Tidings was shut down by the publisher and second, the Tidings former editor, Bert Etling realized Ashland needed a newspaper, founded the online www. Ashland.News and gave the column its new home in January 2022.

I loved every minute of facilitating the column and know it is in good hands and I hope it continues to nourish Ashland as it has me. Below is the letter to the editor as it appeared in the Tidings on Christmas Eve, Dec. 24, 2008 as a Guest Commentary that started the whole thing.

Sally Jean McKirgan

LETTER TO THE EDITOR GUEST COMMENTARY, DEC.24, 2008

In This Season of Love Give Yourself
the Gift of Inner Peace

Having inner peace is as simple as changing your mind. Is there someone who causes you to feel discomfort? Sometimes the thought or memory of this person turns your stomach into knots. That is good! This means you are ready to change your mind. Here's one method that can help.

Can you say with complete certainty that you know everything there is to know, including the past and present about anyone? Do you know every detail of their lives, their fears, hurts, illnesses, challenges or successes? You don't. No one does.

The driver who cut you off in traffic, the slow clerk at the store, the talkative lady at the post office, the guy asking for money for food, the insecure relative or messy neighbor — all are fighting their own hard battles. We don't know what their life is like or what lessons they are here to learn.

If you can drop your judgments and change your mind, you are "choosing peace "right on the spot! To have peace, exclude no one from the compassion, understanding and kindness in your heart.

However, sometimes there are people who continue to annoy. For example, I hate to admit that the 43rd President of the United States has been one of those annoyances for me. I realized however, that disliking him did not make me feel peaceful. Every time I saw his face in the newspaper, a magazine, or being mentioned in a TV talk show, my internal barometer would begin to rise. I could feel the turmoil and judgments running rampant through my mind like scurrying rats at the county dump. To get to the bottom of it I had to look within.

I knew that I was projecting something unrecognized and disliked about myself onto someone else. What was it I disliked so intently? We separate the form of the problem from the content; i.e. the form is war, but what is contained in war? Have I ever gone to war, invaded another country, killing thousands, displacing millions (the form), wreaking havoc on people I don't know? No! Have I ever lied or been deceitful, blamed others or sought to control situations i.e the content? This is where honesty comes in. Sure... but I don't like to admit it. That is why it is called projection.

We project outside and onto someone else whatever it is we do not want to recognize within. "To thyself be true," to quote the Bard! It is not pretty, but next time someone annoys you look at what is contained in the annoyance, not the form it takes, and you will see the projection and then you will stop it and have peace.

Do I condemn myself? Yes, for my faulty thinking. But now that my mistaken projections have been brought to consciousness I can forgive. I must also forgive 43rd as well. In withdrawing my condemnation I am free. Forgiveness offers everything I want because only forgiveness offers inner peace.

Judgments always mean excluding someone from the comfort and reality of love, including yourself. When we condemn we are miserable. Give yourself the gift of inner peace, not only for this season but for six months, a year, and then a lifetime.

Like the Beatles song says, "All you need is love, da dahhh da da dah!" All you need is love, love... Love is all you need!"

Photo Sally McKirgan: Title: Choose Peace – This banner was made for the Ashland "Peace Fence," it was one of many banners made by artists in 2007 and hung on the Rail Road fence to protest the Iraq War. The peace fence banners have been made into tiles and are now displayed in a tile memorial in front of the Ashland Library, Ashland, OR

COLUMNS 2020-21

PIGHEADEDNESS:
TIME FOR SELF-REFLECTION

Stubbornness, mulishness, pigheadedness and obstinacy: My thesaurus has numerous adjectives for what holding your knee on someone's neck for over nine minutes describes. Police Officer Derek Chauvin, (May 25, 2020) was unable to be swayed by onlookers in Minneapolis because he was certain he was right, and no one was going to tell him what to do. He demonstrated what it means to be right rather than happy.

I am sure he is sorry on some level. Maybe at least for being found guilty, but we may never know. I'm sorry for what he did and for people and children of the world to witness that horror. Evidentially it was inevitable and time for the world to know the truth. He showed the incorrigible prejudicial treatment of a black brother and the tremendous fear of authority the police present not only to them but to everyone. He also showed us the stubborn hot anger along with zero ability to step back take a breath and consider what he was doing.

But after reflection and being conscious of my projections, I ask myself if I have been angered to the point of being stupid? Am I projecting my own unregulated anger and dislike onto him? Have I ever done a stupid thing in the name of thinking I'm right? Take the erratic driver on the interstate, weaving in and out of traffic, endangering others. Should I chase him and wave my fist in anger? Have I ever driven erratically? Sure, but I'm not proud of it.

Have I ever pinned someone down and placed my knee on their neck? That is an extreme question to ask, but we need to understand that what others do, we also are capable of—maybe not that extreme, but anger is anger, hate is hate. We see in others what we believe we are incapable of, and it's called "projection." It was a horrid thing, but the ego part of our mind cannot be trusted. Anger cannot be trusted to do the right thing. We need to take our personal temperature. Am I upset? It is up to me to change my mind to calm down and choose peace or at least start to approach the doorway to it. Consciously ask: Do I like how I feel? If

Chauvin could have asked that and allowed himself a moment of insight, he could have changed his life and saved the life of George Floyd.

Stubbornness is a wonderful thing to change, and stubbornness is always of the ego, the false mind. I know policing must be hard and that police are trained to react quickly. Parents are actually in that same position from time to time. We have rules in society of right and wrong: ethics; stupidity is out of control ego. A mind can be calmed when reason, love and mercy are considered: Do I like how I feel? He had plenty of time to change his mind, nine minutes of it. When is enough, enough? Chauvin showed us what happens when the ego is in charge of a locked dungeon trapped mind.

Most spiritual paths and faiths ask us to give up judgment. Jesus: "Judge not, that you be not judged." Buddha: "Do not offend others as you would not be offended." Mohammed: "None of you are true believers until you love for your brother what you love for yourself." When we pre-judge, we separate ourselves from others. It is like holding a knee on their neck. We trap them with our mind. Sure, they can breathe, but we limit them by our thoughts when we could offer acceptance instead. Then we could both breathe. We see them as the ego or false self rather than the Spirit of Light and Love that we all are, and share.

The amazing truth is that the entire world watched and knew what Chauvin did was horribly wrong. The goodness and innate ethics imbedded in the soul knows what's right. By looking at his pigheadedness we can see our own and choose another way. I am hopeful, because it means the many versions of the Golden Rule are STILL alive, well and working in the world. We are reminded in the below quote from the Gospel of Thomas; we need to bring forth our negative thoughts and forgive or they will eventually grow more harmful to ourselves.

> *If you bring forth what is within you,*
> *what you bring forth will save you*
> *If you do not bring forth what is within you;*
> *what you do not bring forth will destroy you.*
> Gospel of Thomas

UNITED VS DIVIDED: THE SPARK OF UNDERSTANDING

"Look once again upon your brother, not without the understanding that he is the way to Heaven or to hell, as you perceive him. ⁶But forget not this; the role you give to him is given you, and you will walk the way you pointed out to him because it is your judgment on yourself." A Course In Miracles T- 25.V. 6:5-6

As of this writing, we don't know who will be President: Trump or Biden, but it is evident from watching the voting in our beautiful country of America, we are pretty equally divided between Republicans and Democrats. United We Stand – Divided We Fall, sorrowfully comes to mind. Is that OK with you? No matter who wins, the condemnation and division will make us miserable until we try to understand it. Understanding brings acceptance. We need to interview each other, meet up online and find out what we have in common. We are the same in so many ways: we live in America, eat and breathe, and we die. We are on the same planet. That should be enough to get us to the table of toleration. What do we love? That is the question.

Besides those basics, there is another profound sameness. Mystics and saints tell us of the spark that is at the center of everyone who is here now, has come or is yet to come. This innocent spark at your center is truth that cannot be extinguished. It carries you throughout your life, a north star, the guide to constant peace within. It cannot die, and you take it with you when your leave this earthly plane. Cherish and engage this spark; it is your touchstone, your Spirit identity, the driving force that guides you to Truth. It is the life force living within and without in everyone. It is a guide for any circumstance that comes, and if consulted, you will know what to do, where to go, and what to say and to whom. There will be no doubts in your holy mind because peace has entered the rock on which you stand as you go forth with the guidance given. Guilt is nowhere to be found in your holy mind. You have nothing that you lack and nothing can put out this eternal life spark; no circumstance is too difficult to understand and no amount of hate can extinguish its holy light.

The spark is in Trump, Biden, Republicans, Democrats, Independents... in everyone. It is in those who protest Black Lives Matter and those who don't. It is in the shooter who kills and the person who is shot. The only difference: the refusal to acknowledge the spark in ourselves is

also in the other. We judge "them" as immoral; we criticize, and demonize others with aversion, we are denying that the spark could possibly be in them. We close our minds, but the spark still burns within all of us. Each of us is responsible for recognizing, enriching, and honoring the spark in ourselves and see it in everyone. After all, it is love.

Love and the evidence it brings dissolves the barriers that cover the spark. Look into a little child's eyes or sweet smile. Hear her call of "Hi" in response to your smile or wave; look into the eyes of your pet or your grandchild; look at the love that comes at you. It is a gift from the spark, the spark we share. Love calls to love and cannot be stopped, destroyed, hurt, or buried.

I don't know what will happen with politics, but we have a life to live. With Covid we don't know how long or well, but we can still live with the fullest amount of love we can give. If you need to go to a protest in the coming weeks, make a sign that says "I love you no matter what." Recognize the spark of love that dwells in the person or persons in the next car, in the kid walking down the street, in the talking head on TV whether or not you agree with them, in the woman in the grocery store line; in the homeless guy with the sign, and in the person standing or sitting next to you. Send love; send acceptance, tolerance and compassion. Open your mind to surround everyone you see, and include yourself. Exclude no one from your love or acceptance, and we will unite and never be divided by politics, religion, or any circumstances life or the world brings. I send Love to all of you.

"As the ego would limit your perception of your brothers to the body, so would the Holy Spirit release your vision and let you see the Great Rays shining from them, so unlimited that they reach to God. It is this shift to vision that is accomplished in the holy instant. Yet it is needful for you to learn just what this shift entails, so you will become willing to make it permanent."
A Course In Miracles, T - 15.IX.1:1-3

WANT TO BE HAPPY?

"You have no idea of the tremendous release and deep peace that comes from meeting yourself and your brothers totally without judgment. ²When you recognize what you are and what your brothers are, you will realize that judging them in any way is without meaning. ³In fact, their meaning is lost to you precisely because you are judging them." A Course In Miracles T- 3.VI.3:1-4

What you think and the judgments you make will make you either happy or sad. The mind is a beautiful thing to change. It is up to you to change it. When the judgmental mind—aka the angry, worried ego—is silenced, there is calmness and unity. Consider taking a deep breath and choosing peace.

During this Covid 19 pandemic, it seems everyone is pretty miserable. Things are not normal or like they were in January 2020. Our lives have been disrupted. How are you feeling? Maybe the better question is "what are you thinking?" Because whatever you are thinking, there is a 99% chance your feelings have something to do with it. I go in and out of worry and depression, but then I remember I'm grateful for those who are on the front lines dealing with it and those who continue to work to keep the world running as well as it is.

The only way to sidestep misery is to be aware of how you perceive the situation. Perhaps a change of mind is in order. You are 100% responsible for what and how you think, judge, understand, and perceive the outside world. We have a choice regarding how we interpret things and situations. If we see something as awful or terrible, we are making a judgment, the ego is in charge, and the mind is fixed. If we can accept that we don't know what something is really about, we can relax and view what goes on around us with an iota of lenience—just a little. We then begin to open the mind to the idea of discernment versus condemnation. With discernment, the mind is open to the idea that we can be tolerant. With condemnation, the mind is closed, locked, never to be swayed, and forever miserable.

I'm thinking of wearing masks as I write this, but it could be anything that disturbs your peace. I think everyone should wear a mask. I don't like them because they restrict air, and I need air, but I wear one anyway. I can understand why someone would choose not to, but I want peace.

So I have to change my mind, on the spot, adding a dash of tolerance and mercy to my thoughts. Just because I disagree, I do not have to allow hatred or anger, thus bringing misery to myself. I can see either love or the call for love. And the call for love is for the other and also to "me, myself and I." My mind needs love and peace as well as theirs. The ego does not have to run and ruin my day, my life. I choose to sideline the dominant ego's thought system and choose charity and mercy and, by the way, make myself happy.

When we give mercy and respect to others, we hold mercy and respect for ourselves too. We don't realize how much needless unconscious guilt we pile on our psyche with righteous judgments and opinions feeling certain we are right. Do I want to be right or happy? I let go of the conviction that I know what's right when in fact I don't.

We like to think that we know it all. But we don't know what our soul needs to experience or lessons we have come to learn, until they arrive at our doorstep. We don't know someone else's lessons either. One thing we can do when we remember we want to be happy is to ask the love within to give us another thought, to help us see things differently. It is imperative to train the mind to choose calmness in the face of horror or fear.

We are responsible for "how we see and how we interpret things and situations." If not at peace, ask the Holy Spirit for a new perception because to looking through the eyes of peace, we will have peace and will be happy.

> *"Across the bridge it is so different!*
> *For a time the body is still seen, but not exclusively,*
> *as it is seen here. "The little spark that holds the*
> *Great Rays within it is also visible, and this spark*
> *cannot be limited long to littleness."*
> A Course In Miracles T- 16.VI.6: 1-3

CHANGE THOUGHTS OF
AVERSION TO MERCY

"Economic factors, personal psychology, impulsiveness, aggressiveness, pleasure, i.e. Utopia all forms of government will fail because people have their hate, their need to be loved and their special interest." Quote attributed to Sigmund Freud in an introductory lecture on Marxism.

What Freud was saying is that if we don't deal with the part of our mind that tolerates hate and thinks its judgments are right and true, no form of government will work. Government does not work, because the ego is in charge, and it is adept at forming alliances and enemies. Nothing seems to change in a world that sees war winding wearily on.

But happily there is something that can change, and that is YOU. What you think, the way you see, perceive and misperceive—that is where change happens. You are 100% responsible for how you think, understand and see. We have a choice in "how" we perceive, seeing either attack or a call for love. If we see attack, we have no peace and we have placed the judgmental ego in charge. If we can view what goes on around us with an iota of lenience—just a little—we begin to open the mind to the idea of tolerance. I'm thinking of politics as I write, but it could be anything that disturbs your peace. I do my share of emailing and calling senators and congressmen, but I can do it with tolerance or avarice. Just because I disagree, I do not have to do it with hatred or anger. I can disagree while holding the idea of respect for the other. The ego mind does not have to run the show of our life. We can set aside the dominant ego thought system and choose charity and mercy.

When we give mercy and respect to the other, we have mercy and respect for our self. We don't realize how much needless unconscious guilt we pile on our psych with askew judgments and rigid opinions: "I am right." We may think we are right, but are we happy? Let go of the thoughts and conviction that you know how the world should run. We need to do what our inner truth guides us, without rancor or separating from the love that you are.

We like to think that we are the wise ones. If we were "King" or "Queen," we could make decrees that would be fair and just for all. We don't know what our soul needs to experience or lessons we have come to learn, until we learn them. We have all experienced being misunderstood or accused of something we did not intend or being unfairly treated. We find forgiveness within when, for instance, knowing how it feels to be unfairly treated, we refuse to mistreat anyone. We can always be helpful, but there are somethings we cannot fix. I cannot fix my alcoholic cousin or the autistic child, but I can still love them. I don't have to judge them, but I can hug them and give them mercy in my mind.

We need to seek for the door in our mind that leads us to understanding and turn from the ego's decree of punishment, fire, and brimstone.

"Then let them go (your judgmental thoughts) and sink below them to the holy place where they can enter not. There is a door beneath them in your mind, which you could not completely lock to hide what lies beyond. Seek for that door and find it.' A Course In Miracles W P1- 131.5.8

I will give the last word to Abraham Lincoln, who said: "My concern is not whether God is on our side; my greatest concern is to be on God's side, for God is always right."

The Winds of War

The Winds of War will be undone,
when all souls refuse the guns!
When they no longer fly the planes,
or drop bombs on those unnamed.
The Winds of War will be undone,
when you and I; everyone,
No longer let our darkness be,
projected out across the Sea.
The Winds of War will be undone,
when love is stronger than hate far flung.
When we can be different and tolerant too,
of others and cultures strange or new.
The Winds of War will be undone
when sane people say: War can never be won!
And nations reject war summons that come.
Then we will have Peace, Brothers as One.
Written on the eve of the Gulf War -1991

THE SPRING 2020 MOON
REMINDS US: "I AM THERE"

Spring is here, and Easter Sunday always follows the first full moon after the spring equinox. That full moon was shining in my bedroom window last night. Passover was April 9, Easter Sunday the 12th, and Ramadan on Friday April 24. However, the only ones feeling "spring like" these days are the birds and the daffodils. Aren't they lucky to not have to stay inside or six feet away from each other because of Covid 19? Thankfully, we can visit them with thanks for their songs and yellow loveliness. There will be no religious gatherings indoors this year, and I know many will miss this spring ritual. I must admit that Easter has always left me feeling sad. Even dressing up or hunting for eggs, bunnies and candy never took away the unhappiness.

I felt relief after I began studying the spiritual, psychological, non-dual, mystical and metaphysical book, "A Course In Miracles," where the concept of resurrection is more prominent than crucifixion, because as eternal beings our soul never dies. The body dies because we are mortal. Being mortal, we have a split mind with an ego that crucifies ourselves and/or others non-stop with doubts, judgment, war and attacks. Jesus in the Course told the scribe, NY Columbia Presbyterian Psychologist Helen Schucman, that he is our equal and elder brother: "The miracle is a sign of love among equals. Equals should not be in awe of one another because awe implies inequality. It is therefore an inappropriate reaction to me. An elder brother is entitled to respect for his greater experience, and obedience for his greater wisdom. There is nothing about me that you cannot attain. I have nothing that does not come from God. The difference between us now is that I have nothing else. This leaves me in a state which is only potential in you." Text Chapter 1.II.3.4-12.

He assures us that he and the Holy Spirit are always there for us. "I go before you because I am beyond the ego. Reach, therefore, for my hand because you want to transcend the ego. My strength will never be wanting, and if you choose to share it you will do so." (Chapter 8.V.6 7-9.) If we take his hand, he is there to share his strength. He is the Christ, but so are you and I and everyone, and we are all equally loved by God, whether we accept it or not.

At this time, we need a strength that is not of this world. Many brave people are in the trenches, the doctors, nurses, medical staff, sick patients, relatives, friends; and you and I are with them. The hand of strength, grace, and faith is there for us. It is waiting by your side, with arms ready to hold you up and kissing the top of your head when you pray. That love is made exquisitely clear in the poem "I am There" by James Dillet Freeman. He is sometimes known as "the poet laureate of the moon," because two of his poems are on the moon. "I am There" was taken by astronaut James B. Irwin in 1971 and "Prayer for Protection" by Lunar Commander Buzz Aldrin in July 1969. Freeman's poems of assurance are circling above us on the Easter moon, blessing you and me and everyone on our beautiful blue planet.

I am There

Do you need Me?
I am there.
You cannot see Me, yet I am the light you see by.
You cannot hear Me, yet I speak through your voice.
You cannot feel Me, yet I am the power at work in your hands.
I am at work, though you do not understand My ways.
I am at work, though you do not recognize My works.
I am not strange visions. I am not mysteries.
Only in absolute stillness, beyond self, can you know Me as I am, and then but as a feeling and a faith.
Yet I am there. Yet I hear. Yet I answer.
When you need Me, I am there.
Even if you deny Me, I am there.
Even when you feel most alone, I am there.
Even in your fears, I am there.
Even in your pain, I am there.
I am there when you pray and when you do not pray.
I am in you, and you are in Me.

Only in your mind can you feel separate from Me, for only in your mind are the mists of "yours" and "mine."

Yet only with your mind can you know Me and experience Me.

Empty your heart of empty fears.

When you get yourself out of the way, I am there.

You can of yourself do nothing, but I can do all.

And I am in all.

Though you may not see the good, good is there, for I am there.

I am there because I have to be, because I am.

Only in Me does the world have meaning; only out of Me does the world take form; only because of Me does the world go forward.

I am the law on which the movement of the stars and the growth of living cells are founded.

I am the love that is the law's fulfilling. I am assurance. I am peace. I am oneness. I am the law that you can live by. I am the love that you can cling to. I am your assurance. I am your peace. I am one with you. I am.

Though you fail to find Me, I do not fail you.

Though your faith in Me is unsure, My faith in you never wavers, because I know you, because I love you. Beloved, I am there.

The Prayer of Protection

The light of God surrounds us;
The love of God enfolds us;
The power of God protects us;
The presence of God watches over us;
Wherever we are, God is!
Learn more about James Dillet Freeman at www.unity.com.

Sally McKigan Title: The Seven Continents:
Loving Mother Earth –Mixed Media

THE PEACEMAKER – DEGANAWIDAH AND THE GREAT TREE OF PEACE

The legend of Deganwidah and the great tree of peace is remarkable since it is instrumental in the shaping the American Bill of Rights, the U.S. Constitution, the U.N. and governments across the Atlantic. Briefly here is an outline of this powerful true story.

Deganawidah, a 15th Century Peacemaker was born into the Huron tribe, a tribe where young men found their identity in war. His early life was marked by difficulties. His grandmother learned of a prophesy foretelling that he would not be favorable to his tribe. Legend says, several times she tried to kill the baby but he always ended up back in his mother's arms. He grew up giving advice on peace and friendship, saying it came from the Great Spirit and introduced the concept of the "New Mind." He was rejected with scorn. Like St. Francis, animals loved him and birds sat on his shoulder.

He left home as a teenager on an epic journey to spread the message of brotherhood among all peoples. On his journey, he encountered hunters who warned him of a cannibalistic man. He converted this man who was overcome with grief because his family had been killed by a warring tribe when he saw how revenge and grief caused excessive damage to the creative spirit of life. He developed a grieving ceremony using condolence beads to transform grief into love then forgiveness. This ceremony is used by some tribes to this day. He met Hiawatha (not to be confused with the Hiawatha in Henry Wadsworth Longfellow's poem) and asked him to be his spokesperson since Deganawidah had a stutter. In his travels he met an Erie tribeswoman, Jigonhsasse, and convinced her to stop feeding the warring raiders who came by her home. She accepted his message. He called her the Great Peacewoman and the Mother of Nations.

The next challenge was to approach the Mohawks who were the fiercest tribe. According to the legend the Mohawks refused to join him unless he performed a feat to prove his power. He climbed a tree hanging over Cohoes Falls and told the warriors to cut it down. They saw him disappear into the rapids but the next morning they found him sitting at a campfire. The Mohawks realized his great power and became the founding tribe of the Iroquois Confederacy.

Next he approached the fierce Onondaga's and an Indian, Tadodaho, who was twisted, evil and vindictive. He screamed at the Peacemaker's so they traveled to the Cayuga's who accepted his peace vision. Eventually three Chief's accepted his New Mind concept and traveled to convince the angry Tadodaho, but were rejected so they visited the Seneca's who joined them.

Then representatives of the four tribes went to Tadodaho again. They were rejected, but they did not give up; they offered him herbs to heal his twisted body, wampum offerings and remedies for his broken spirit. Slowly they transformed him. They invited him to join them as keeper of the Council Fire of the five nations, to serve instead of terrify. It was a great honor. To this day the Onondaga chief heads the Council Fire of the five tribes. The spiritual leader takes the title Tadodaho. Deganawidah always used his peacemaking skills, since what good is peacemaking if it requires retribution and war. The term chief or sachem means "he does good" and indeed has to do good, in order to qualify for the role.

The tribes then gathered at Onondaga Lake, where they planted the Great Tree of Peace, a large tall white pine. Its four white roots would travel to the four directions spreading peace. Warriors were asked to bring instruments of war including warring thoughts and bury them where they would disappear forever. This is where "bury the hatchet" originated. A great Eagle symbolizing the Great Spirit was placed on the tree top to "be on the lookout" but also to watch for the enemy that lies within. The five tribes: Mohawk; Seneca; Cayuga; Oneida; Onondaga were joined later by the Tuscarora into the Iroquois Confederacy, called Haudenosaunee. These tribes resided (and still do) in New York, Pennsylvania, Eastern Ontario and the Great Lakes area.

Per Wikipedia: This confederacy influenced the United States Constitution and Anglo-American ideas of democracy, as recognized by Concurrent Resolution 331 issued by the U. S. Congress in 1988, which states in part:

> "Whereas the original framers of the Constitution, including, most notably, George Washington and Benjamin Franklin, are known to have greatly admired the concepts of the Six Nations of the Iroquois Confederacy; Whereas the confederation of the original Thirteen Colonies into one republic was influenced by the political system developed by the Iroquois Confederacy as were many of the democratic principles which were incorporated into the Constitution itself..."

We owe Deganawidah (his name respectfully is not spoken aloud, but he is referred to as, The Great Peacemaker) a charismatic, courageous spiritual master and prophet, a great debt of gratitude. You can read the Constitution of the Iroquois Confederacy on Wikipedia.com as well as other historical books. I recommend the book: "Manual for the Peacemaker, An Iroquois Legend to Heal Self and Society" by Jean Houston with Margaret Rubin.

Sally J. McKirgan

Above the Mess

When you think you've fallen, into the pits of hell,
And with a heavy heart, ask: "This where I dwell?"
When doubts assail the mind, fear rants and raves about,
Wondering where to turn, you want a quick way out.
Rise above the ego mess, go to the lap of God.
It's where you're loved, far above the doubts, the fog.
You're not the one below, feeling distress and pain.
Now rest in soothing peace, for God will never blame.
Do not identify, with fears and cares below.
This is your heavenly home where the soft winds blow.
When held in forgiveness, problems always dissolve.
You are the Christ, a Son of God, everything is solved.
Remember it's possible, to rise above the mess.
And when you do, all worries disappear in the mist.

COLUMNS 2019

GOOD POLITICS IS AT THE SERVICE OF PEACE

I learned recently about the "World Day of Peace" when a friend loaned me the video "Pope Francis, A Man of his Word." If you are ready for some inspiration, I highly recommend it. The 52nd World Day of Peace was January 1, 2019. Pope Francis's message was: "Good politics is at the service of peace." He made several points, but the first was "Peace be to this house." What he was saying was "peace for our family, our house, our communities, our country, our continent and, importantly, our common home, our world.

As our nation's politics take the stage for the next year we might keep in mind his thoughtful recommendations. He expanded on several pertinent points by suggesting that "charity and human virtues along with service of human rights and peace be the basis of politics." He suggested those running for office should recall the "Beatitudes of the Politician," which were proposed by Vietnamese Cardinal François-Xavier Nguyễn Văn Thuận, who died in 2002. Here they are:

Blessed be the politician with a lofty sense and deep understanding of his role.

Blessed be the politician who personally exemplifies credibility.

Blessed be the politician who works for the common good and not his or her own interest.

Blessed be the politician who remains consistent.

Blessed be the politician who works for unity.

Blessed be the politician who works to accomplish radical change.

Blessed be the politician who is capable of listening.

Blessed be the politician who is without fear.

He suggests that every election and re-election, and every stage of public life, is an opportunity to return to the original points of reference that inspire justice and law. "Good politics is at the service of peace. It respects and promotes fundamental human rights, which are at the same time mutual obligations, enabling a bond of trust and gratitude to be forged between present and future generations."

Watching it was like a breath of fresh political air. If we look for and vote for those who from all appearances seem to hold these values, we would have leaders that we, the world and future generations, deserve.

He also brought up political vices: dishonesty, self-service, corruption, exploitation and denial of rights and plundering of natural resources for the sake of quick profit, to name a few. Good politics inspires and promotes participation of the young and trust in others and fosters confidence that we can all work together for the common good. Politics at the service of peace finds expression in the recognition of the gifts and abilities when everyone contributes his or her gifts to help build trust especially in our times marked by mistrust and rooted in fear of strangers.

Regarding past wars and the strategy of fear, he says to threaten others is to lower them to the status of objects and deny their dignity. Escalation and uncontrolled proliferation of arms is contrary to morality.

Lastly, he calls for a great project of peace and reminds us of the Universal Declaration of Human Rights adopted after the Second World War: "Man's awareness of his rights lead to the recognition of duties; the rights are the expression of personal dignity and their recognition and respect by others." Peace entails a conversion of the heart and soul; it is both interior and communal; and it has three inseparable aspects:

1. Peace with oneself: Rejecting inflexibility, anger, and impatience by showing "a bit of sweetness towards oneself" in order to offer "a bit of sweetness to others."

2. Peace with others: Family members, friends, strangers, the poor and the suffering; being unafraid to encounter them and listen to what they have to say.

3. Rediscovering the grandeur of God's gift and our shared responsibility as inhabitants of this world as builders of the future. When anyone suffers, we are all affected. God sees with his heart. Even the atheist shares the same love. Maybe that's the only common bond we all have, the bond of God's love. Other than that, we are free, even free not to love Him. To read the entire message: http://w2.vatican.va/content/francesco/ en/messages/peace/documents/papa-francesco_20181208_ messaggio-52giornatamondiale-pace2019.html

THE ANTIDOTE TO HATE
IS NOT MORE HATE

"The symbols of hate against the symbols of love play out a conflict that does not exist. ²For symbols stand for something else, and the symbol of love is without meaning if love is everything." A Course In Miracles, T - 16.IV.2:1-2

I woke up this morning with that headline in my mind. The antidote to hate cannot be more hate because that creates fear and worry. Can hate be fought with more hate? The letter to the editor that began this column appeared as a guest commentary on Christmas Eve, 2008, titled: "In this the Season of Love, give yourself the gift of inner peace." It was my antidote to the hate I felt at the time towards President Bush and the Iraq war debacle raging in the Middle East.

For years I searched for inner peace by looking for peace in the world, but to no one's surprise, I found that peace is an inside job. The world is neutral. We can see peace or hate depending on what is in our mind. What do I see and think, how do I feel, and what do I believe to be true? What are my perceptions, and are they tainted by years of false training? For example, in the first grade I was told by my teacher not to walk around holding the hand of the new little "black" girl who had just come to school. She was the first black person I had ever seen; I thought she was amazingly beautiful. My teacher told me it was inappropriate! She was teaching division, hatred—a false training. And I wasn't in Alabama but Washington State! Hate hurts the hater. Hatred causes stress, guilt, division, anger, anxiety, fear, ossification, resentment, obstruction of blood vessels, inflaming the brain, heart, joints, arthritis and other degenerative diseases. Just watch TV ads to see all the remedies offered!

We observe hate and fear "out there," but the solution is not to add further hate to the equation. I was an antiwar demonstrator but could never hate the other side. We can demonstrate against something with peace in our hearts if we hold a "we are the same" thought because that IS the truth. We do have the solutions because they beautifully emerge in our society, like the answer to homelessness with the Medford and Ashland communities developing solutions with little houses and winter shelters with caring (loving) volunteers. The answer is within each of us.

The person who is driven to kill and shoot at a school/synagogue/ mosque is suffering. Find whoever suffers (him/her) and hold them; include them; invite them to lunch; hold out your hand; or give a pat on the back. Try to connect even with a smile because he/she is hurting, feeling rejected and full of a resentment that will ultimately explode until they obtain a gun to kill someone or maybe themselves. What is the antidote for this suffering that I can offer? I don't always give money to people asking at the store, but I do give a smile or a wave. Everyone is hurting at some level, not just the homeless. We have the right response within if we ask and let it arise.

We have been programed or "carefully taught" as goes the song in the movie "South Pacific": "You've got to be taught to be afraid of people whose eyes are oddly made or people whose skin is a different shade; you've got to be carefully taught." If we observe our judgments, they are probably from a past learning, but we have the power to no longer accept, believe or live by them.

We have answers for the antidote. For example, Rabbi David Zazlow's congregation at the Havurah visited the Masjid Al Tawheed mosque in Talent and visa versa. I know the United Congregational Church of Christ has done the same. Jewish and Christian congregations cross-pollinate as well. Small gatherings are not intimidating. I've seen posters for many community gathering opportunities. We need to meet, engage, enlighten and demonstrate acceptance and inclusion for everyone in all the Rogue Valley communities.

The publisher of the Medford Mail Tribune, Stephen Saslow, in his May 5th editorial said: "If we're ever gonna survive," called for a Band-Aid to violence and asked for suggestions. What are your ideas? Let's put our hearts and heads together because we have the answers, the antidote:

"Peace is stronger than war because it heals.
War is division, not increase.
¹⁰No one gains from strife.
A Course In Miracles T-5.II.7:8-10

Refuse to Hate

At times it's so easy to blame and hate.
Project on a brother, never relate.
The pain is intense when hate is inside
All peace is lost, no place to run, to hide.
You have the power; change your holy mind.
What you see is judgment; ugly; unkind.
Change the hate and say: "This I do not choose"
You want to see the light! What can you lose"?
Closing your eyes: surround pain in love's light,
Ask God: "Please help me see through darkness bright."
Hate changes to love when looked at with Him.
Give it to God who will never see sin.
He will cleanse it, sending it to Heaven.

Peace and happiness come with new vision.
Do not harbor guilt; be kind to your mind.
It was a mistake! Now ego resigns!

THE PAIN OF LONELINESS
– THE MINDLESS SUPREME COURT IN OUR HEAD

"I would see you as my friend, that I may remember you are part of me and come to know myself." A Course In Miracles, W p1. 68.

In today's political climate, I sometimes feel like there is a Supreme Court Justice sitting at the bench in my head. Actually, a Supreme Court Justice is probably more thoughtful than my ego ruminations. And the ego does ruminate when I let it go on and on without realizing what it's up to. What is the point of continually judging others or circumstances? Let's face it: it is fun being the judge! We sit on the "bench" and make one rapid fire decision after another. "She's really skinny; he's arrogant—too rich, too poor, so stupid, or homeless." True, we are taught to discern from our earliest years, primarily for our safety or protection. Watch out for that hot stove, fast cars, certain religions, dogs that bite, a steep cliff, poison oak, stranger-danger, or deep water. After all, this world is not a safe place. It is not Heaven, but it could be—but more on that later.

We grow up, and our fearful monkey mind has been well trained to live in fear and to judge everything we see. The problem is that we believe our thoughts to be true. Even when we know better, the ego continues to use judgment to separate, divide, and fragment ourselves because ultimately the purpose is to keep us far away from loving and accepting. The ego is afraid of love. We cannot love something we have previously condemned. So the ego puts us on our guard, and the outcome is loneliness. If we continue to live in a tight and constricted closed mind where we can hardly breathe, we are certainly not free nor are we happy. We end up exclusive rather than inclusive, in exile, alone and longing for fresh air and freedom. We also long for the expansiveness of an uncluttered Mind.

We were never been told when we were young that we have a mind with a capital "M." We needed to be controlled. However, we finally come to recognize our True identity is Mind and Spirit, and gradually we cease to run on automatic as a puppet of the ego, or reside in the small "m" mind. We remember that we can choose again, what and how we will think. We stop believing everything we think is true. We watch and change our thought patterns and attain more inner peace. When we watch our thoughts with detachment, the gig is up on the ego. We are aware of how it works, and we start to wake up. In becoming the objective observer, you remove yourself from the "bench." What a relief. Just say: "I don't have to believe this thought, it is not necessarily true." We no longer believe every judgment that crosses our mind. Observe it and just let go. Letting go is forgiving! If you hang onto a thought, ask: "What is this for?" If un-loving, then it's to keep love away. A thought is separation whether negative or positive. For example, "I wish I had her figure" is still a thought of separation because it separates me from her, and I judge myself as lacking somehow! That's not love.

Imagine what a thought that accepts light, gives love, unity, and peace does for you. Imagine what it does to your immune system, your body, and the chemicals in your brain. Kindness and loving thoughts heal because we are holding LOVE, the great healer, in our mind.

What a relief to give up judgment. We can even disagree with someone and yet decide not withhold judgment because beyond the disagreement our ONE identity is Mind and Spirit. I may not agree with you, but once I decide to look at you with LOVE, all former disagreements and judgments dissolve and we dwell in the ONE healed Mind.

> *"The light that joins you and your brother*
> *shines throughout the universe, and because*
> *it joins you and him, so it makes you and him*
> *One with your Creator."*
> A Course In Miracles, T - 22.VI.15:1)

COLUMNS 2018

EASTER PEACE: "ALL ARE WELCOME HERE"

"Hate has no business here. We stand with our Muslim Community Members. We stand with refugees and immigrants in our community. All are Welcome Here." (This flier was posted on the front door of the First Presbyterian Church, Ashland, OR, Easter morning 2018. It was also placed on doors and windows of many businesses in town.)

This is what greeted us upon entering the First Presbyterian Church in Ashland a few weeks ago. With open arms and hearts, it bids the entire world to enter. To me, it says no one would be denied entrance regardless of belief, race, social status, or whether or not they believed in God. The poster is in nine languages, so whatever your native tongue, most likely it is there.

My husband wanted to visit the Presbyterian Church because he recalled enjoying it as a young boy in Iowa. First he went by himself. I said if he liked it, I would join him to see what I thought. After I saw the sign on the door, I realized why he felt at Home, because I surely did.

This was unlike the Church I visited as child, where not everyone would have been welcome. One Sunday when I was about seven, I looked out the window at the beautiful green trees, and in a brilliant instant, I knew that God was not hateful and that we were not the sinners the fat red-faced preacher claimed we were. I grew up wondering if solace and peace could be found anywhere in the world, because it wasn't in Church. After a search of various thought systems and spiritualties, I did find peace, and with it came the realization that God Is the greatest of mysteries, and is Love and only Love because where else could something as beatific as Love commence, unless it originated from outside this insane war-weary world.

Easter with the fuzzy bunnies, candy eggs, and colored jelly beans has never covered the elephant in the room: The Crucifixion. The symbol of the resurrection implies that while bodies die, the spirit is eternal.

We cannot prove that the spirit never dies, but there have been many near-death experience stories, like Dr. Eben Alexander's book "Proof of Heaven" and many others that strongly indicate life after death. We come as spirit; we inhabit a body, but we learn we are more than a body.

We are born into a dualistic world of opposites: life and death, love and hate. We are programed by our family, culture, and society, which all serve to "entomb" us like the Easter story. The tomb protects us, but it also functions to deceive and keep us separate. We accept the programming of our individual "tombs" and wonder why we continue to feel depressed, persecuted, or alone. We feel bereft of love and at the same time afraid of it.

We are afraid of love because the ego or shadow part of our dualistic mind judges and finds fault with things. You cannot love something you've previously condemned. As soon as we think we are happy, we are not. How long have you been happy after you bought the new _____ ? (Fill in the blank.) There is always something more. We walk a lonely road in the dark woods of separation, seeking but never finding, and at times we feel crucified.

In the Easter Story, Jesus was certainly hated, but he refused to return it and offered only love and forgiveness. Overcoming hate, then, is our resurrection from the tomb. We are resurrected from the programming of the dark tomb we inhabit, and like Jesus, we offer tolerance, love, and—yes—forgiveness too. We roll the rock away and free our lives and our spirit from the tight grip of egoic judgment and hatred. Our mind then opens to the clarity of healing light. We come here to overcome the programming and refuse one unkind thought about anyone or anything anywhere. All hate is of the ego; all love is of God.

Like the Church, we place a post-it note over our heart: "Hate has no business here." We then wake each day choosing peace and embracing each other as the loving One Family of humanity we are.

The #HateHasNoBizHere slogan was first tweeted by Common Roots Cafe, a member of the Main Street Alliance, in Minneapolis Minnesota, along with the message "All Are Welcome Here." The Main Street Alliance, headquartered in Washington, D.C. with small business members across the country, works to serve as the voice of small business in America on the most pressing public policy issues across the nation. Their message now? America's diversity is its greatest strength. Permission granted by: The Main Street Alliance.

Red Bi-Plane: Steel Sea

Red bi-plane diving nigh: hard steel sea,
Scaring the wits out of little me,
Riveted and standing very still,
Alone on the beach, what a big thrill.
How confident, bold and fearless too,
Performing stunts over smooth steel blue,
I was destined to see you that day,
To remind me: We are spirit not clay.
Wish you had landed, given me a ride.
All terror would retreat by your brave side.
Secretly you energized my soul,
Me: Never daring or ready to go.
I could be fearless, limitless like you,
Joyfully sky ward, to God, we two!
Thank you pilot for facing off fear
Does angelic protection hover near?

JUST DO IT" AND ASHLAND'S WORLD PEACE FLAME

"Believe in something…even if it means sacrificing everything." Colin Kaepernick, former San Francisco NFL football quarterback.

The above statement resides at the heart of every conscientious objector as well as those who have marched for a cause and or been arrested for civil disobedience. Former San Francisco 49er, Colin Kaepernick, should come to Ashland on September 21st for the World Peace Flame lighting ceremony. Peace is for him and for anyone who yearns for the sweet hope residing in the symbolism of this flame. Cheers to the Culture of Peace Commission founders who had the vision and worked diligently to bring it here! They Just Did It!!

I've never met Colin Kaepernick, who drew the ire of the U.S. President and others because he had the nerve to kneel for justice for his black brothers who have been brutally killed, targeted, and mistreated by police. My heart went out to him at the time for his brave act of civil disobedience. It does not matter that he and I are from different races or generations. Nothing matters when we realize people are treated unfairly and that the hand of justice is not fair for all – especially if you are black. He was not listened to nor was he understood. Neither was Socrates or Jesus.

The National Anthem is a piece of music. The American flag is a piece of cloth. They are symbols that stand for courage, honesty, freedom, justice, and bravery—everything he demonstrated. In my heart, I will go to the lion's den of the sports stadiums of the world, to hold his or other hands, for peace, mercy, and compassion for those brutalized or treated unjustly. And many are, like the parents and children separated at the border because they entered this country seeking asylum. The symbols of America are for all people, all religions, all ethnic groups, politicians, police and immigrants included. No one is excluded. Who doesn't understand the word ALL??

If the government that oversees the promise of America is unjust or ineffective, what is one to do? Civil disobedience and non-violence are smarter and intellectually more advanced than threats, violence, and bombs. What would Jesus do? What would Gandhi do? What would Martin Luther King do? Kaepernick loves his people and his country enough to sacrifice himself for its promise. That is the courage that compelled him and now the Nike Corporation as well. They Just Did It!

And sacrifice he has. He may never play football again, but the bullying did not bend him. It bent the NFL. As Huck Finn said after contemplating the "sin" of not sending a letter that would return his slave friend Jim back to his master, "All right, then, I'll GO to hell"—and he tore it up. Huck did the right thing for his friend. Kaepernick has seen his share of pain and hell.

We all encounter pain in life. Most of us know grief and loss. Why wouldn't we want to ease his pain? Why wouldn't we want to ease ours? Symbolically, if we can join our Mind with the idea of mercy and offer understanding, then gentleness will surely appear on some mystical level that we may not understand, to help him and us. So how do we ease pain? Take Tylenol, have a drink, maybe two or three. Go to a concert, a movie, a football game; pray, meet with friends, make an appointment with your therapist, or...? We seek various distractions to lessen the existential pain of existence. Look at the supplement counters and the variety of prescriptions advertised on TV.

On Friday September 21, (2018) the World Peace Flame will be installed at Thalden Pavilion by the Culture of Peace. This flame has been installed at sites around the world. It represents the spark within us that KNOWS what is right and will not be bullied into submission. The spark challenges us to awaken and unite with the One Mind, that links us to God, to all souls present, past and those yet to come. As we gather to proclaim our commitment to peace, let the light of this shinning flame remind us of the spark within each of us that we all share that comforts all pain.

I ask but this; that you be comforted and live no more in terror and in pain.

Do not abandon Love. Remember this; whatever you may think about yourself, whatever you may think about the world, your Father needs you and will call to you until you come to Him in peace at last. A Course In Miracles S-3.IV.10:5-7

CHRISTMAS 2018: PART I, "WHY CHRISTMAS?"

Years ago, our youngest son, after being put to bed on Christmas Eve, looked at his Dad and inquired, "Why Christmas?" It was a perceptive and honest question from his sweet little three-year-old mind. How would you answer him? It is a good question to pose to our grownup selves. We rush about planning and making lists, driving ourselves crazy, or going on the internet to find the best deals. We fret over what to give to whom and whether they will like it.

And then we imagine them opening it up, and we watch carefully for the expression that comes in that twinkling moment. Maybe that "instant" is our gift! That shining twinkling moment when we made someone happy, see them smile and gasp with surprise, with an "Ooooo" and words of thanks, and hopefully not a groan.

My husband's father loved chocolate-covered cherries. Every year we gave him a box. Finally, one year he opened the gift and said, "Oh no, not cherries again." That was the last year we gave him cherries! How many of us have opened presents that we definitely did NOT like but managed to feign appreciation by falsely showing we "love it" and have "always wanted one?"

Back to Why Christmas? Well, it is all about Jesus and his Birth Day, right? It seems that Jesus and his teachings of love, inclusion, and non-judgment are not relevant at times. A few years ago, I was sitting in a restaurant reading a book about Jesus. The author had put the beautiful face of Jesus smack on the cover. A gentleman stopped to ask what I was reading. I smiled at him, silently closed the book, and showed him the cover. You would have thought I was pointing a machine gun in his face! He was absolutely horrified, shocked! His eyes were big, brows shot up, and he looked like someone had hit him with a stun gun. His adverse reaction was palpable. He said "Oh" and hurried away.

Where does that reaction come from? For over 2,000 years the world has had Jesus to deal with. Over the ages, scholars, sages, saints, wise men and women have written about him and various faiths have their concepts and judgments, but where does the "aversion" come from, especially when he innocently asked us to Love one another? What's wrong with that?

One reason could be that since the Bible claims he Jesus is "God's ONLY begotten son," where does that leave the rest of us and the poor horrified man? We know families that have a favorite child whose attributes outshine everyone else, the gifted child. Could it be an unconscious jealousy that stretches through the ages with resentment and feelings of the rest of us being unloved? It can fester throughout the centuries or in a lifetime. How many of us, deep down, feel as adored as that "Away in the Manager" baby?

So how do you explain Christmas to a small child? Of course, we have that Jolly Old Elf, Santa Claus, who gives gifts to good children, and if, Heaven forbid, they haven't been good, the threat of guilt with a capital "G" lands on their little psyches. We also give to those we love and help those in need, donating food and furthering Jesus's suggestion to love thy neighbor. Next week in Part 2, I will go into what we could have said to our small child if we had known then what we know now. Isn't that always the case? In the meantime, what would you say to "Why Christmas?"

Painting Watercolor Title: World Peace – Religious Symbols Join in Peace - As Christmas Ornaments - Sally McKirgan –all art available at: sally-mckirgan.pixels.com

CHRISTMAS 2018: PART II, "WHY CHRISTMAS"

"The sign of Christmas is a star, a light in darkness. See it not outside yourself, but shining in the Heaven within, and accept it as the sign the time of Christ has come." "A Course In Miracles," T-15.XI.2:1-2)

When our young son asked his innocent question mentioned in Part I, "Why Christmas?" I'm not sure what my husband said, but it did surprise him. We attended Church as children, but with adulthood came agnostic tendencies. We didn't see much evidence of a supreme being. It was 1973, the Vietnam War was raging, with protests and plenty of injustice and starvation in the world. How could God allow such misery?

We loved Christmas with our two young boys, Santa's visit, singing carols about Jesus's birth, yet sadness somehow prevailed. That sadness eventually led to the search for the deeper meaning in life. The existential "WHY are we here" was surfacing in our minds and hearts. After several years of exploring a variety of religions and spiritual paths, we became students of the spiritual, psychological, metaphysical, non-dual, mystical book, "A Course In Miracles."

Helen Schucman, the scribe of the Course, said she heard the voice of Jesus dictating the Course to her over a period of seven years. In Chapter 1. He said:

"You (the sonship) are a perfect creation, and should experience awe only in the Presence of the Creator of perfection. Equals should not be in awe of one another because awe implies inequality. It is therefore an inappropriate reaction to me. An elder brother is entitled to respect for his greater experience, and obedience for his greater wisdom. He is also entitled to love because he is a brother, and to devotion if he is devoted. It is only my devotion that entitles me to yours. There is nothing about me that you cannot attain. I have nothing that does not come from God. The

difference between us now is that I have nothing else. This leaves me in a state which is only potential in you." A Course In Miracles T - I.II.3.3-13

Jesus, our equal elder brother, is devoted to us. He says we are the same regardless of any perceived differences, because we "think" we have separated from God. We haven't, but we need to let go of the ego part of our mind distracting us from where God's memory is found.

"The memory of God comes to the quiet mind. In quietness are all things answered, and is every problem quietly resolved. ACIM T-.27. IV. 1."

The difference between Jesus and us is that we still have an ego. Our mind is split between love and fear. Jesus is the example. We have the power to choose the ego or Jesus and or the Holy Spirit within. It is a lifetime goal, maybe many lifetimes, simple but not easy. Are we tolerant and loving; are we attracted to peace or repulsed like the poor shocked man in Part 1 last week?

"This Course does not aim at teaching the meaning of love, for that is beyond what can be taught. It does aim, however, at removing the blocks to the awareness of love's presence, which is your natural inheritance." ACIM Introduction.

Why are we here? To remove the blocks barring love from our hearts. We learn lessons in from our lives, we withdraw projections or judgment placed on others. We let go of the past, the cherished grievances; we forgive by looking honestly within and seeing we are all the same, no one to blame including ourselves.

"Can you imagine what it means to have no cares, no worries, no anxieties, but merely to be perfectly calm and quiet all the time?" ACIM T-15.I.1.1

The part of our Mind still connected to God compels us to awaken. We grow weary of the ego and its guilt. The Course says God, being only love, does not judge or condemn. We can no longer blame God for wars and problems we create following the ego.

If we had been students of the Course when our young son asked "Why Christmas?" we could have snuggled him and his brother on our laps and assured them: "You are loved as dearly as the baby Jesus because the same light placed in Jesus by God is also in you; God loves everyone equally; baby Jesus grew up to be a wise man who is in your Mind and heart as God is; be kind. See God's love and light shining in everyone."

Jesus' Christmas gift to the world is non-judgmental, all-inclusive eternal love and light. You can't buy it. It is yours, you inherited it. When you accept it; you live it, you give it. The Christmas Star of light dwells within you. Have a Merry Christmas.

You are Forgiven

You're forgiven; you have done nothing wrong.
It's time to recall God's home where you belong.
There is no sin, mistakes you've made a few.
Nothing you've done can keep God's love from you.
You're His perfect Son, believe it so or not.
Know God's Truth: You are Forever in His thoughts.
Forgiveness comes from the Holy Self in you.
Heaven's open door has always been there too.
Close your eyes; seek the quiet Self-that's real.
This is what you are; Love inside will heal.
Ask Holy Spirit's help; He never resists.
He's there with the answer that will not miss.
Change your mind and the old beliefs dissolve.
Now you understand; all things are resolved.
With forgiveness learn God's Love is so pure.
No matter what, it's always been secure.
You're forgiven; you have done nothing wrong.
We know Heaven is where you now belong.
Dedicated to Shawn Jason 1970-2013

COLUMNS 2017

LEARN TO ACKNOWLEDGE PROJECTIONS FOR INNER PEACE

His Holiness The Dalai Lama has said on occasion that we will not have peace in the world until we have inner peace. Many spiritual paths help us become aware of the duality of the split mind containing opposite thoughts of love or fear. The thoughts of the false self, the ego, is not who we are, but it runs the world and our lives until we begin to awaken to see it for what it is.

On that note, I awoke one morning recently with the following thought: "Our 45th President is operating from his personality, the false self. This false self, a mask, is not the reality of his true identity. He is not that any more than my false self is who I am." It was an "Ahh ha" moment, because I've been aware that I certainly lose my peace when I watch him on TV or read the newspapers.

To delve further, it is our thoughts and judgments that determine whether we have the inner peace about which his Holiness speaks. We can believe our thoughts or not, that is our choice. Judgmental thoughts come from our perceptions and then are projected "out" and seen in someone else rather than accepted in ourselves. That's called projection.

Some history, per Wikipedia: *"Psychological projection is a theory in psychology in which humans defend themselves against their own unconscious impulses or qualities (both positive and negative) by denying their existence in themselves while attributing them to others. For example, a person who is habitually rude may constantly accuse other people of being rude. It incorporates blame shifting. In 1841, Ludwig Feuerbach was the first enlightenment thinker to employ this concept. The Babylon Talmud (500 CE) notes the human tendency toward projection and warns against it: "Do not taunt your neighbor with the blemish you yourself have."*

The term "Projection" was conceptualized by Freud. He considered that, in projection, thoughts, motivations, desires, and feelings that cannot be accepted as one's own are dealt with by being placed in the outside world and attributed to someone else. What the ego repudiates is split off and placed in another. "To gain some peace then, we gradually understand the projections we have placed on others by looking inward to see where the "offense" is. As we honestly look, we may recognize aspects of similarities, if not in the exact form but similar in content. We thus awaken because we look (not always easy to do because we prefer denial) and accept by ever so little, and in doing so, we in effect forgive ourselves and the one we are projecting onto. We are the same! We look honestly and see it in our self and with draw the projection. We changed our mind. Inner peace is the prize! That's forgiveness! For example, I may not send "tweets" attacking or insulting others, but I may harbor judgmental thoughts. They may not be the same, but still they are judgments. Freedom is looking without judgment, but when we do judge (and we will), don't feel guilty for having judged! The ego will try and lay on the guilt, but instead laugh, chuckle, or smile at the folly of the crazy world. Eventually the ego will dissolve.

Why go to this trouble to acknowledge projection? If we keep it buried in our unconscious, it will eventually emerge in anger, envy, and hate. In making judgments, we are in effect depositing our "darkness or shadow" onto someone else. That may make us feel better for a while because we got rid of it, but the downside is the residual blotch of guilt, a gift the ego neatly places in our mind. We are addicted to judgment; after all, we've been doing it since we threw our bottle across the room or whenever we decided we didn't want to obey our parents, which echoes the authority problem we have with anyone from bosses to God.

Whenever your peace flies away, whether you're a Democrat, Republican, or Independent, your ego has taken charge. You are pushing love away. Many non-dual teachers say it is reminiscent of the first thought of separation; the separation from God and from love. Whether you believe that or not, one thing is sure: we do feel the lack of love at times. Everyone needs and wants to be loved; movies and TV ads are full of it.

We gradually learn we are One; we are the same; we all have the same false ego and the correction of the higher self. Know this as you head out the door with your sign, standing as a peacemaker or a protester, but at the same time exclude no one from your love. We can still disagree about policies while holding the hand of the other who sees things differently.

Maybe put a few red hearts on your sign to send the subliminal message: Love is the reason I am here. Now we are no longer staring at the shadows on the walls of Plato's cave, because we move to the Light by holding the hands of all brothers and we trust and have faith that knowledge and peace will lead the way. We are in good hands, we lack nothing, and everyone is loved.

> *"Not one light in Heaven but goes with you.*
> *Not one Ray that shines forever in the Mind of God*
> *but shines on you. Heaven is joined with you in your*
> *advance to Heaven. When such great lights have*
> *joined with you to give the little spark of your desire*
> *the power of God Himself, can you remain*
> *in darkness? You and your brother are coming*
> *home together, after a long and meaningless journey*
> *that you undertook apart, and that led nowhere.*
> *You have found your brother, and you will light each*
> *other's way. And from this light will the Great Rays*
> *extend back into darkness and forward unto God,*
> *to shine away the past and so make room for*
> *His eternal Presence, in which everything is radiant*
> *in the light."* A Course In Miracles T- 18.III.8:1-7

Photo: "Mt. Shasta's Heart" Mt. Shasta, CA

BEING: "I AM" PURE CONSCIOUSNESS

"The mind of an enlightened human being is flexible and adaptable. The mind of an ignorant person is conditioned and fixed."
Ajhan Sumedho, "Don't Take Your Life Seriously," Buddhist Publishing Group

A friend recently loaned me the above book by Ajahn Sumedho. Ajahn, ("teacher" in Pali) was born Robert Karr Jackman, July 27, 1934, in Seattle. He is the senior Western representative of the Thai forest tradition of Theravada Buddhism. A bhikkhu since 1967, Sumedho is considered a seminal figure in the transmission of the Buddha's teachings to the West. During the Korean War he served for four years, beginning at the age of 18, as a United States navy medic. He graduated in 1963 with an M.A. in South Asian studies from the University of California, Berkeley. (Per Wikipedia.)

From what I have gleaned from his book of over 30 essays on wisdom practices, we now find ourselves with the opportunity to either be adaptable or be fixed. I don't know about you, but I've been fixated on politics, our nation, and world conditions since the January changes in government. Chaos and change happen in our lives, and that creates nervousness and anxiety, the opposing poles of inner peace. Ajahn says the world is "just the way it is!" Accept! We are not at peace when we judge anyone or when we feel superior or inferior to others. We constantly compare what is "here and now" with "how it should be." As babies we are not born with a self-view that is developed over our lifetime. We therefore become a "created concept" and ignorant until we realize the pain we suffer and seek relief.

Whenever self-concepts turn to good, evil, smart, stupid, etc., we are still in ignorance. You are not that! When we choose, we can acknowledge innate pure consciousness to receive wisdom. Wisdom operates through the marriage of awareness joining with consciousness. Suffering is one of The Four Noble truths in Buddhist tradition. Judgment is suffering. As we become aware of pure consciousness, judgments shift and soften.

The ego personality says, "I like this or I don't like that." It is my choice then: should I get caught up in the annoyance, suppress it, or try to change it? I know I want my way, but can I be assured that will bring me peace? Until I can accept the world is just "like it is" and that "what is just - is," I am the one choosing to suffer. Buddha called it Dukkha.

When you say "I AM pure consciousness uncreated," your mind is at rest. Say it slowly with eyes closed. Say it slowly with eyes open. Pure consciousness does not have a sex, nationality, or a world view. It means, I AM—not a permanent body, but rather I am eternal, consciousness. Consciousness is behind awareness, like the Buddha, or Christ and other Masters.

Contrast this with the impermanent, unsatisfactory "not self" that we think we are. The idea of "me and mine" is created out of ignorance and separation from pure consciousness. The personality and life circumstances always change. You don't stay the same person, because the ego personality is reactive. Old age is another seeming failure, but pure consciousness does not age. Awareness transcends the conditioned ego state. If we continue to give our allegiance and beliefs to the ego rather than to our natural pure awareness, we will suffer—until we tire of it.

Sumedho's solution is to seek refuge in awareness and pure consciousness. As we look at national and world conditions, be aware and say, "So it is." Awareness is constant, and pure consciousness stands behind in a circle of light. Consciousness is stainless; it cannot be contaminated. It reminds me of His Holiness the Dalai Lama, working for peace yet staying in pure consciousness throughout the tumult of his life.

To quote Sumedho: "*Wisdom, then, is the ability to discern the difference between consciousness without attachment and consciousness with attachment. If I am attached, then I get lost in my attachment without awareness and I become what I am attached to. When I recognize pure consciousness with non-attachment, however, there is just this simple reality of attentiveness here and now. This is the path of non-suffering.*

You actually recognize it is no longer a matter of holding to an idea of enlightenment. All of that drops away and there is just recognizing and operating from the natural, pure state of your being here and now is totally trustworthy."

Perhaps we will become enlightened as insanity propels us to approach pure consciousness: non-attachment vs. pure hell. As the months and years unfold, this practice connects us to the wisdom and peace available at the center of our One Luminous Being.

SEE EITHER LOVE OR THE CALL FOR LOVE

The United Nation's International Day of Peace is Saturday, September 21, 2017. Imagine all the people in all Nations of the World stopping for 24 hours to think about Peace! Peace with other countries, counties, family, and neighbors! We don't have to hate. Do we? Do we have to judge or condemn? If a trusted adult tells us that others are offensive, we may tend to believe them, especially when we are young. We are taught and most of us believe and accept what we are taught, but we certainly don't have to. For example, my mother was prejudiced against a certain race. I had played with some of these kids at school and liked them, so I did not accept her belief, but I did obey her and not go to their houses. As it turned out, my sister married a man of that race, and lo and behold, she changed her mind. A mind is a beautiful thing to change. Mom was a lovely person, but she accepted her conditioning and passed it on. It reminds me of the Roger's and Hammerstein South Pacific song, "You've Got to Be Carefully Taught." But we do not have to accept society's teaching. Hate is a choice.

Could it be that a part of our mind enjoys hate? Think about how you feel when you are in the "hate" emotion. Doesn't it make you feel strong and powerful and, above all, right! Years ago, I worked in an office with a young man who was mentally impaired. He was from a rich family, and he annoyed me and I disliked him. Looking back after years of spiritual work, I wondered what that was about. I think I hated him because he reminded me of my own mental impairment. I always thought I was stupid! We project onto others that which we have inside yet do not want to see or admit. It is projected out and seen elsewhere, but heaven not in me! When I think of him now, I send love to him wherever he is, and I believe his soul receives it. I know mine does.

Hate and anger are harmful to the hater in many ways. Have you ever tried to be nice when you didn't want to? What does that type of mental activity do to the brain/body? Check out the Every Day Health website, https://www.everydayhealth.com/news/ways-anger-ruining-your-health/.

From various studies, this site documents the side effects of hate and negative emotions on the heart and brain, creating stress hormones, which in turn cause depression and even inflammation. The ego is the "Master Judge" in our mind that runs our lives until we understand that we are in fact miserable and see through the fog and decide to change our thoughts and choose peace. The ego uses projection and hate as a roadblock to love. We choose the ego until we decide not to. However, we have a choice because we are a decider!

Hate is offensive. When we see angry people, it is very ugly and distasteful. We feel a churning inside. TV and movies offer a heavy diet of violence and hate, an onslaught to the nervous systems. To be honest we need to admit that the hate we see reflected in the world outside is also within. If we can admit that, then we are no longer in conflict and it dissipates. Instead of "pulling the wool" over our eyes, we just look honestly, and in looking, it dissolves. If we don't fight it or put up obstacles, we avoid a pile of buried guilt being placed deep within the psyche to emerge unexpectedly, which it will. Look squarely at the angry person, and see either love or a call for love. Try it. You will access a place of peace. You do not need to say aloud "I love you"; merely think it. The mind is choosing love instead of the ego's automatic response of disgust or hate. Their anger is their momentary condition but not their reality. In giving love, you receive it. You don't know if or what you will "do or say," because the situation will depend on wisdom from the higher Self. But you can always think love.

I love this quote attributed to Abraham Lincoln: "To defeat an enemy, make him a friend." You could also say "To defeat an angry person, recognize it is also within, and see either love or a call for love."

If I exclude love from others, I am excluding love from myself. With compassion, we no longer condemn. We are the same; we, all people, and nations need peace. The Spark of the Divine is within everyone, so I challenge myself to look for it.

*"In many only the spark remains, for the Great Rays
are obscured. Yet God has kept the spark alive so that
the Rays can never be completely forgotten. If you but
see the little spark you will learn of the greater light,
for the Rays are there unseen."*
A Course In Miracles T- 10.IV.8:1-3

You can't get away from us, Mom!

I know life was hard at times; because I was there to see!
I watched you work hard to keep us from the grip of poverty.
I left home at eighteen years; you were always in my heart,
We talked on the phone for years, I never felt far apart.
Forgive me from leaving you and moving away from home,
My heart was always with you, no matter where I should roam.
You may take a journey too, and think you leave us behind.
But wherever you may go, our love will seek and find.
You can't get away from us Mom, in this Universe of Song.
Our Father has a safe place where we all really belong.
And it is at Home with Him, In Heaven where we are One.
We come here for one reason, to forgive and love all Sons.
I know with all my heart, we are together in his Love,
And we still where we never left: At Home in God's pure Love.
You can't get away from us Mom!

WHENEVER YOU MAKE
A JUDGMENT.

"We can never obtain peace in the outer world until we make peace with ourselves."
His Holiness the Dalai Lama

To make peace with ourselves we exclude no one from our love, practice kindness, and watch the judgmental thoughts. Watching and withdrawing thoughts is a gift, not only to you, but to our family, community, and the entire world.

For example, when you make a judgment about anyone, make it about yourself as well. This is hard because the idea about "seeing something out there" means I do not want to "see it in here." For example our President makes judgments about people all the time. I may think it is terrible, but don't I do the same thing—maybe not the exact same thought or form on Twitter or TV, but how about judgments in general? He vocalizes his judgments, and we most likely keep ours to ourselves. Some of us were taught that it's OK to think it, but if you can't say something nice, don't say anything. Or keep quiet and look intelligent, but open your mouth and look stupid? But even by thinking the judgment, it still is in my mind even if I never say it. It still is separation, condemnation, and attack. Yes, we all have judgments, and that is why the Dalai Lama says we can never obtain peace until we make peace within ourselves.

To make peace within, all we need do is be conscious of the judgments. We "see" as we look inward and say "yes, I've thought that or I've done that," and by doing so you are not caught up in the misery of blame, condemnation, or separation. Voicing judgments is cruel and hurtful. We call it bullying, and we may never want to hurt anyone, but what are we doing to our own mind but filling it with thoughts of division? We start judging as babies, the minute we refuse to eat some of the food our Mother feeds us, and we cry and fuss but we outgrow it...if we want peace.

We all have egos. The ego separates, and the way to peace is to watch it, the thoughts it generates, and in watching it, the ego is gradually seen for what it is and diminished. There is nothing wrong with telling someone they are wrong as long as it is done from a place of love and not hate. It is no longer hate when we cleanse it of separation that is, seeing it as being in them and not in ourselves! We can say yes, we may have done that or thought that, but we see that it did not come from love. Only loving thoughts reflect Truth. We learn to work from that non-egoic place of love, within the mind as a grown up, the peacemaker, and we never attach ourselves to the outcome. We don't know if our actions will be understood. We let go of our attachment to the outcome. If we are attached, we will not have peace.

It is no longer "hate" when we see "it", hold the hand of love and see our projections. We are the same. We have the same ego (the false self), and we have the same holy mind. We have the same hate. Do I want to see the obstacles and judgments, or do I want to see past those distractions? This road to enlightenment, is not easy going, but you are worth it.

By watching the judgmental thoughts we cease being miserable. When our scattered mind stops automatically judging everything that comes into sight, including past memories and future fears, we are more present. Ask yourself, "Who is in charge of my thoughts and my judgments?" We have a choice to look at them, accept them for the distraction they are, and see they are not TRUE. They are not true if they are not extending love.

Apologize America – Accept Equality!

Live the honor that you claim to have.
Be the open heart that you claim to be.
Have the courage to uphold the treaties.
Everyone is created equal. Accept!
They are endowed by our Creator God
With certain unalienable rights! Accept!
That among these are life, liberty and
The pursuit of happiness! Accept!
Uphold your stated Promise America!
Everyone is accepted and loved by God
Regardless of skin color; religion, race
LBGTQ or? How about it? Accept!
Are we free and equal or not?
Apologize America! Live your promise.

COLUMNS 2016

INTERNATIONAL PEACE DAY: TAKE YOUR TEMPERATURE

The International Day of Peace, sometimes unofficially known as World Peace Day, is observed annually on 21 September. It is dedicated to world peace, specifically to the absence of war and violence, such as might be occasioned by a temporary ceasefire in a combat zone for humanitarian aid access. The day was first celebrated in 1982 and is kept by many nations, political groups, military groups, and peoples. (Source: Wikipedia.)

This year the theme is "The Sustainable Development Goals: Building Blocks of Peace," a worthy goal. However, in 2017 or the near future, the theme could be "The Sustainable Individual: Take Your Peace Temperature." The U.N. could lead the way in encouraging the practice of personal peace and promote the daily "hygienic" practice of taking one's peace temperature, like brushing teeth or combing hair. Are you a peacemaker or a troublemaker? We know Global Warming is heating the planet, bringing dire predictions, but something that we can do something about is the temperature of our mind. For example, on a scale of 1 to 10, with 1 being peaceful, what is your temperature today? If encouraged to perform the task of accessing our daily inner temperature, we would look inward: am I happy or sad; upset; what can I forgive or accept; what do I need to do; take a walk in the park; write an apology or thank you; what am I thinking and should I believe it; what am I judging; projecting; and can I find it also within myself so that I can let it go?

In taking my temperature, I am responsible for looking at my thoughts and changing them if they cause pain, grief, or misery of any kind. Who or what part of my mind is running the show that translates into my judgments and thoughts? Unless I choose differently, it's the ego. I don't have to believe every thought or the drama attached to it that can escalate to a war pitch in my mind. When we are aware of the escalation and how we feel and think, we can say: "Do I want this thought; is it true? Can I refuse to believe it or see it another way?" Question every thought, and when a judgmental thought crops up (and it will) say: "Oh there's the ego again—no big deal." Merely look and let it go. If I take the time to look within and name the annoyance or the judgement, I must acknowledge that it is also in myself; it has to be. Otherwise, I would not see it out there. Understanding this, I can let it go or see it another way. All condemnations are from the ego, a master in projection if we let it be chairman of our thoughts.

Salvation from the ego is within your powerful mind. You are the decision maker and can put the controls on the ego. Switch channels. Go to the sanity within and say, "I choose peace; I want to see this differently." Find the "mute" button and turn off the ego insanity. Maybe carry a small symbol in your pocket as a reminder to choose peace. This practice of watching the mind will reduce the ego. It is imperative for inner peace.

The ego is not your friend. You are a loving mind, a higher Self, a Spirit, you are innocent, and have done nothing wrong. As we become less identified with the ego, the quiet truth will emerge from the Love within the One mind we share. We live in a world that screams of distraction and misery, especially with the current war in the Middle East, refugees flooding Europe, and the general election. But there is always something screaming at us. A mind at peace will find the loving thing to do when called upon, and if we don't buy into ego doom and gloom, we will see clearly what the right thing is. No longer living as a puppet of the ego, we take our inner peace temperature daily, allowing the love within to be projected outward to do the good it will. Take your inner peace temperature next September 21, and have a nice day!

> *"Your goal was darkness, in which no ray of light could enter.*
> *And you sought a blackness so complete that you could*
> *hide from truth forever, in complete insanity. What you*
> *forgot was simply that God cannot destroy Himself. The*
> *light is in you. Darkness can cover it, but cannot put it out."*
> A Course In Miracles T -18.III.1:4-8

OUR HALLOWEEN IDENTITY: GOBLIN, GHOUL OR ANGEL

At Halloween, we can have fun exploring our various inner "creature features" and play "let's pretend" for one night. At some point during our lives, many of us wonder who we really are. Some question and search more than others, and maybe that's a curse, depending on how you look at it. But the basic human question is: who am I and why am I here? Halloween is fun because we can be someone or something else and escape from whatever it is we think we are. And besides, it is fun, so why not?

Deep down we know love is the essence, the core of our conscious being. We all have a Dr. Jekyll or Mr. Hyde split personality lurking within the ego self we've constructed to deal with life to live in the world where we find ourselves. We can be kind one minute and hateful the next, depending on which voice we are heeding. But that double identity still keeps us from realizing the light and the love that is our truth.

You are not the double identity your ego would have you believe. The ego is merely a thought in your mind. It is a false thought system, however. If you let it run your life, controlling every thought and action, you will be miserable and wonder why happiness is elusive. The ego is not who you are, it is not your friend, and it will never make you happy as you continue to seek and never find. It can make you feel superior or inferior. It does not want peace, love, or harmony. It tells you that you will be happy if you do such and such. It does not want you to be truly happy because that would put it out of business. The ego is a lie.

A wise person said, "We are spiritual beings having a human experience." We will be happy if we remember to accept the Light and the Love within us that is farbeyond any false ego thought. The mystics tell us we are the light of the World! We are complete and healed and whole, loved, loving, and lovable. We need to let the realization of our true identity sink in, and that will happen when we change our thoughts and practice mindfulness. The calm beauty and grandeur of your true identity will reveal itself gradually. As you allow the fog to lift, things will bother you less and less. You gradually train your mind by not believing every little egoic thought that arises. Eventually the happiness of heaven, where loneliness does not exist, will dawn upon you.

You inherited Love. It is a gift, a present within you that you discover when you become present. You are the creator of Love, but it came with you from the factory. Love just extends. No one lives who does not have it. That would be impossible. Whenever you have a loving thought or extend love to someone, you are shining the light you came with. Just watch a baby (after their diapers are changed), and remember their sweet love is glowing at you—and connecting with yours. Mystics say it is God shinning in this world from one mind to another.

Whenever you see Love, you are seeing your True Self and your inheritance. To be happy, extend the Love within you to everyone and every living thing—your friends, enemies—and exclude no one.

When you are kind and loving, your journey and your classroom will be peaceful and joyful. Since love is internal and comes from the eternal, it can never run out. It is like the magic pot of pudding in the child's story that boils over unceasingly—impossible to halt or stop!

Remind yourself of the limitless love that is your true identity everyday by saying:

I am the light of the world. I am Spirit, I am Love and I am Loved, Therefore I extend Love to all whom I meet. I walk in Love and there is nothing to fear.

Numerous daily repetitions will allow the belief set in your mind. You may not believe it, but that does not mean that it is not true.

So, dress up this Halloween—be anything you want, but at the same time, KNOW WHO you REALLY ARE!

*"How holy am I, who have been given the function
of lighting up the world! Let me be still before my
holiness. In its calm light let all my conflicts disappear.
In its peace let me remember Who I am."*
A Course In Miracles W pl - 81.1:1-5)

Painting Sally McKirgan Title: Fly Like an Eagle

CHOOSING PEACE DURING THE POLITICAL SEASON

Politics! You've probably noticed lately that during this presidential election season we are cheering or jeering one candidate or the other. We choose sides, and it may seem ridiculous but it looks like we actually enjoy disliking one of the candidates, or maybe both? Of course, we need to vote, but choosing peace during this process is a challenge.

We find ourselves gnashing our teeth over what they say or don't say, and it can be fun or unnerving depending on who said what. I think we like disturbances on some level. Some of you may remember the "dustup" over Medford's pedestrian and bicycle bridge over Barnett Road a few years ago. There is always something going on, like the recent choice of a sculpture for the gateway of Ashland, or the store owner who displayed a controversial book in the front window of her store. We like controversy because it makes us "feel" something: upset, offended, judgmental, or alive, and we think we are right and everyone else is wrong. It is either a "love it or hate it" at the time, but thankfully, time will move on and memories can fade. This will happen with the current political season, but only if you don't attach yourself to the outcome.

Attachment and disappointment could keep the rumination going for years and decades to come. Attachment is problematic. We want "things" our way. When we don't get what we want, we suffer, especially when we hold on to the grievance. Why hold on? Do we like to suffer? That must be the case when we hold the anger or grudge and are unwilling to let go.

We can get involved in issues but we will retain our peace when we let go of the outcome. Holding on to the outcome is a recipe for suffering. Do your best, work with good will and a courageous mind-set and learn how to meditate, if you don't already, so that not getting your way will roll like water off a duck's back.

The book "Relaxation Revolution" by Herbert Benson, M.D., (2010) tips: https://www.bensonhenryinstitute.org.

1. Sit quietly in a comfortable position

2. Close your eyes.

3. Relax all your muscles, beginning at your feet, and progress up to your face and top of head. Keep them relaxed.

4. Breathe through your nose and focus on your breathing. As you breath in and out, repeat the word "ONE" silently to yourself in a slow but natural rhythm. This focusing of the mind is called a mantra. You can use any word or sound, but be sure it is neutral.

5. Continue this calming practice for twenty minutes, and if distracting thoughts come up, gently repeat the word "ONE" to settle the mind.

6. Do not worry about whether you are successful or not.

When you finish, sit quietly with your eyes closed. At first, I had a pencil and paper nearby to jot things I deemed important to remember because the mind does not quiet down easily. Eventually it will. Practice meditating at least once a day and twice is better, but wait a couple of hours after eating a meal.

You will reach a deep level of relaxation, and you won't care about politics, the outcome, or the election. The benefits are immense, and peace is your prize no matter who wins.

> *"There is a hush in Heaven, a happy expectancy, a little*
> *pause of gladness in acknowledgment of the journey's*
> *end. For Heaven knows you well, as you know Heaven.*
> *No illusions stand between you and your brother now.*
> *Look not upon the little wall of shadows. The sun has*
> *risen over it. How can a shadow keep you from the sun?*
> *No more can you be kept by shadows from the light in*
> *which illusions end."*
> A Course In Miracles T- 19.IV-A.6:1-7

A HOLIDAY GIFT: QUIET YOUR HOLY MIND

How many of our spiritual leaders, from Oprah, Deepak Chopra, Byron Katie, Marianne Williamson, His Holiness the Dalai Lama, to Eckhart Tolle, tell us that when we quiet the mind we will attain inner peace. Do we want a quiet mind? If so, are we willing to make the effort? Maybe the real question is: Am I worth it? There are many methods, but they all involve watching the antics of our thoughts and letting them go rather than "attaching to believing" them. It can be a challenge, but the gain is indeed worth the effort. Inner peace can be fleeting, but the more and more the mind is quieted, it becomes more attuned and attracted to the gain. Like the mouse in the maze that discovers the sugar cube, we train ourselves. Thus, mind training or mind watching brings the delightful rewards of snippets of inner peace.

One thing is sure—we can't have a quiet mind if we are constantly judging people, events, and the things we see or think we see. Judging is the ego's primary goal, and it keeps us in a state of estrangement, which leads to loneliness and the gift of guilt.

We will have more and more peace when we refuse to judge. You don't have to! Just look, accept others—everyone—all of them, friends, relatives, the guy who cut you off in traffic, and if the mind seeks revenge (i.e., judgment), just say "uh uh, not today." Drop the inclination (or maybe it's a secret desire?) to go on a rapid judgmental rant. You ARE in charge of what/how/why you think. Peace will be prevalent when the separation and judgment cease.

One way to stop the judgments, once they have been made, is being aware and "looking" at them squarely. Above all, refuse to judge yourself for making the judgment. If you do, it is ego self-attack and the ego has you by the throat.

When you judge yourself (good or bad), you are making the ego seem powerful and real. It isn't! It isn't real because it does not come from love. It is not WHO you are. If we continue to hang onto the judgment, hate, and grievance or upset, we are giving the ego power and keeping it engaged. Hate and judgment are war, the opposite of quietness and peace. What is the purpose of keeping the grievance ALIVE? What does it serve?

Judgment is purposive. It keeps us entrenched in the ego and, quite frankly, in misery. With the ego and our judgments in the forefront, we are imbedded in the world of division, which keeps the idea and the reality of love from arising in our holy mind.

It seems senseless, but the judgments only serve to keep love away. It boils down simply to being afraid to love. When we accept our identity as being love and spirit, then we are free. The need to assert our individuality would be nil. We keep the ego and our judgments in order to stay in the world and be FAR away from God…away from our reality, which is Love.

World Peace is attained by each of us looking and undoing the hatred (judgments) within. We expose the darkness by taking gentle steps. Joy is finally recognizing you have done nothing wrong with these false silly judgments and GUILT is GONE! You have a Holy Mind whether or not you think you do. Let it shine outward, and give the Holiday gift of love and acceptance to everyone and all living things and life forms in the World and the Universe.

COLUMNS 2015

YOUR BEAUTIFUL BENEFICENT MIND

There is a blessed relief that washes over us when we feel loved. A blue jay recently bounced onto a flimsy oak branch outside my window with an acorn in its beak. It flew to the ground and hopped around the garden looking for just the right place to store it. A few minutes later it was sitting in the pear tree, sans acorn. I know it is storing food for the future, but it is also taking care of my little yard and our planet too. I feel loved and I appreciate its beautiful blueness. I see its actions extending beyond its everyday duties for the good of everything. Maybe tomorrow I won't feel loved, but if I can stop and recall the blue jay, and the goodness inherent in you and all living things, the love will return. I am reminded of Love's Presence daily if I look for it rather than the opposite.

We see the bitter struggles and the aching sense of being on the outside looking in when we watch the news and the Middle East refugees trying to find a place of respite for themselves and their families. But there are struggles here as well: addictions, homelessness, combat PTSD, suicides, and the Black Lives Matter campaign. All worthy causes and all people need love, acceptance, and peace. If we can let a thought of pure joy fill our mind, for just an instant: Respite Is, Peace Is! We care, we weep, but weeping doesn't help. A thought of LOVE does. It has recently been proven that a mind can "pick up" thoughts, and we have sense perceptions we are not aware of. But just because we are unaware does not mean they are not there.

In the book "The Source Field Investigations," author David Wilcox calls it consciousness transfer (pg. 33). He describes it thus: *"Dr. Charles Tart of Berkeley, CA conducted an experiment where he gave himself electric shocks and then attempted to 'send' his pain to another person who was the 'receiver.' The other person, in another room, was wired up to measure heart rate, blood volume, and other physiological signals. Tart found that the receiver's body did indeed respond to the shocks through such things as an increased in heart rate and a decrease in blood volume, but the receiver had no conscious knowledge of when Dr. Tart was sending them."*

Many spiritualties speak of the One Mind. From the spiritual, psychological book, A Course In Miracles, *"You are being blessed by every beneficent thought of any of your brothers anywhere. You should want to bless them in return, out of gratitude. You need not know them individually or they you."* A Course In Miracles T 5.in.3:1-3 The mind is very powerful. Loving, beneficent thoughts sent out into the world, to people we want to help, to our neighborhood and town, can be "received" on some level. Can the sunbeam be separate from the sun? Can an idea be separate from the mind that thinks it? Peace is giving beneficent love, and in so doing, we also feel love and know we are not separate or alone. The cure for loneliness: Send love to someone. Use it to go to sleep at night.

Be cognizant of the ego part of the mind that does not believe we could possibly be connected, to each other, want peace, or for that matter, love. The ego loves to exclude, separate, condemn, and judge. Watching politics is proof enough. However, the ego does not represent Truth. Love and forgiveness are as close to Truth as we can get in duality. Let the world "go," and realize its whims or yours do not last for long. Identify with your true Self/ Spirit/Soul /Mind that is connected to everyone. God/Love is not distant but found within. There is a blessing in Unity churches which ends with the words "Wherever I am, God is." You can also say, "Wherever I am, Love is."

> *"How holy are our minds! And everything we see reflects the holiness within the mind at one with God and with itself. How easily do errors disappear, and death give place to everlasting life."*
> A Course In Miracles W pl -124 2. 1-3

TIRED OF VIOLENCE

How do we get rid of violence in our communities? We take steps to rid ourselves of the violence in our hearts, minds, and souls.

Looking at ourselves honestly and seeing the violence we harbor within is a huge step towards ridding ourselves and society of its egoic tendency for anger and callousness. It is natural to get angry at times, especially when something does not go our way, like getting cut off in traffic. Usually, when we recognize the anger, we feel stupid and ashamed. If we can monitor our anger and recognize that it comes from the false self that is not who we are, we forgive and let it go. We need to be honest with ourselves, however, to see the anger, realize it is the cause of so much guilt, and then heal our mind with the love that is contained in every heart and mind. We have a choice: whenever anger arises, recognize it (don't deny it), see it, say this is not who I am; then say "I am love," and let it go. Love enters and peace is regained. We are all the good guys, we are all bad guys, but love will guide us.

One way we can be helpful to our neighbors (and ourselves) is to take some thoughtful action to realistically reduce violence in our society. Here are three ideas:

One: Refuse to watch the violent programs showing the glorification of guns and violence on television programming. If we stop watching, there will not be any money in it. Years ago, the advertising of hard liquor and cigarettes was taken off TV. Violent programs including guns are just as dangerous as liquor and cigarettes. We as a society are being neglectful of the youth of America when we let guns and violence be front and center.

Why do young men kill and why are they so angry? They are being horrifically mistreated by the "entertainment" industry. They are being neglected and fed a diet of violence on TV, in video games, and in movies. Violence, murder, and crime are considered entertainment because they make money for TV stations, advertisers, writers, producers, actors, filmmakers and their production companies, and more. The TV and movie industry will claim that violence came first and that they are mirroring society, but society is mirroring them. They will ask "which came first, the chicken or the egg?" That question has no answer, but that doesn't mean that feeding America a diet of violence is ethical. However, we could stop watching programs with violence and or stop purchasing the advertisers' products, it will hurt their bottom line.

Two: Fund Mental Health programs generously. Not only fund them, but put mental health on the front burner. Former Senator Patrick Kennedy has written a book about his family and the "secret" struggle of alcoholism, addiction, and the effort it takes to hide behind big smiles and hurting hearts. All families either have or know someone who is struggling through the mental health programs in this country, which are "funded" in a miserly fashion. In Jackson County here in Oregon, there are a so few beds at the Hospital psychiatric ward that people are turned away. Mr. Kennedy has bravely come forward to expose the stigma associated with mental illness and why it is as important as Cancer or Heart Disease. Mental health problems fester; they affect our society; they don't go away, and we all suffer mass murder because of it. Here is a link to Senator Kennedy's website, where you can learn more about his work: http://www.patrickjkennedy.net/.

Three: No guns of any caliber for anyone under the age of 21. We know that a recent killer named Chris Harper Mercer was age 26. When did he first own a gun? If it had been unlawful for him to have one or to go to a shooting range until age 21, perhaps he might have found a better path. According to a recent CNN pole, 27 mass shootings have happened since 1949. Out of a 66-year period, 14, half of the mass shootings, occurred within the last ten years. What does that tell you about violence piped into our homes via TV? Eight of these crimes were committed by young men in their twenties.

Back to looking at violence in ourselves—how many of the young murderers were treated with love, compassion, and kindness? I'm sure their parents tried their best, but did schools educate them, and was therapeutic intervention offered? Did the health system care for their psyches and minds as much as their bodies?

We won't be able to banish guns and violence from our society until we banish the anger within. We need to bring our guilt to the light of love and be willing to open our minds to "hear" answers from all segments of our society to solve the problems, join hands, and together choose peace and have faith that we will figure this out.

THE ANSWER IS FORGIVENESS: LOOK; WAIT AND JUDGE NOT

What does guilt have to do with me? I recall having immense feelings of guilt, but I had not done anything horrifically wrong to match that immensity. I learned later in my spiritual journey that I had unknowingly chosen to be separate from God (we all have), which was the cause of the guilt, but more on that later. It was the feeling of guilt drove me to become a seeker. Was there a balm for it, and if so, where and what? The spiritual path that I follow states that the only balm for guilt is forgiveness, and through forgiveness the ego is finally undone.

Until we finally look at the ego, we cover it over with positive thoughts and self-esteem training, and we deny and reframe things in our minds so that we feel better for a while. However, the ego still jabs and will have its way until it can be seen for what it is: Disturber in Chief. However, if we give it power and "fight" it, it becomes bigger. That is the ego's goal....to keep us off balance, mindless, and in conflict with someone and something, anything. That is why wars continue to be fought. The ego is happy as long as there is a struggle.

The answer is to quietly watch, observe, and ask for inner guidance to see through the fog of the ego. And this is critical: Do not judge it or yourself. Become defenseless and refuse to believe its lies. If you don't buy into it, it is sidelined. There are three aspects of forgiveness:

1. Look.

2. Wait.

3. No judgment.

1. Look - try the following exercise. What are you currently feeling guilty or uneasy about? Write them down. We push guilt down, deny it, or justify it. The more we deny, the more it will "come out" somewhere. Repression does not work. Perhaps you have several "little" items that

have been hanging around in your mind for years. Go ahead, write them all down. You don't have to show it to anyone. Burn the paper if you are worried. At least "you" have been honest and faced them by looking. Looking plays a big part in undoing the ego.

The ego does not have your best interests at heart. It can and will sabotage you. For example, perhaps you are in a hurry and are rude to the store clerk or made a rude remark to someone, even to someone you love. What will follow at some point will be the thought "You were rude." That is the ego in action. You did something stupid and feel guilty. If you did something you are not proud of, why not apologize? See how the ego hates and resists that idea! Even if the person is no longer in the area or living, you can still apologize to their memory. "I know I treated you badly, I apologize to your Spirit, please forgive me _____." In so doing, you are acknowledging that you are not the ego. The Self who you really are is Light and Love. In acknowledging you are freeing yourself from the ego, the black cloud of guilt ruining your inner peace, dissipates. Always ask your inner guidance, the voice for truth, the Holy Spirit to help you look at everything especially the upsets. Looking is a big part of forgiving!

2. Wait - the ego does not like to wait. When something from the past is triggered the ego offers a thought, or something to do or say, but don't do it. It is just a thought, the ego egging you on! Clear your mind and Wait. Wait and ask for guidance, be patient an answer will come.

3. No judgment - do not judge yourself. We live in a world of duality—right and wrong, black and white, guilty and innocent, and on and on. We really have no way of knowing what is right and wrong in many situations. If you are upset the ego has taken the lead. If you judge yourself for being rude to the clerk, the ego is pulling the strings of your mind. Judgment is an ego trap to make you feel guilty. Say: "I will not judge myself right now. I'm waiting for Truth."

We need to train ourselves to watch and not follow the ego thought system. The ego sits on the Judge's bench and judges everything that crosses its path. You are not the ego but a Mind; the decision maker i.e. The Decider. You, the Decider, can choose between the ego or the inner voice for peace. When on automatic the ego runs the system. But, as the Decider, ask "How can I see this differently?" Then listen for the small still voice of Truth. Remember: When you choose, the ego will lose!

> *"Forgiveness, on the other hand, is still,*
> *and quietly does nothing.*
> *It offends no aspect of reality,*
> *nor seeks to twist it to appearances it likes.*
> *It merely looks, and waits, and judges not."*
> A Course In Miracles| W-pII.1.4:1-3

NATIVE AMERICAN WORLD PEACE AND PRAYER DAY

On June 20 and 21, (2015) join Native American Lakota Chief Arvol Looking Horse, the founder of World Peace and Prayer Day, and other spiritual leaders at the 20th annual event at Howard Prairie Lake.

How often do we pray? Some often, some never, but when in trouble... everyone. Prayer is an act of asking for something we desire. Praying does not have to be to God, but it does mean going within and acknowledging innermost longings. What do we really want, lack, or seek answers to? Heaven knows living in this world is challenging. The opposite of praying is denial or escape. We escape by buying toys and looking for diversions, anything to replace some of the bitterness of life. Maybe having a glass or two of wine or beer or using some marijuana will join the list of methods for escape. Getting "high" is escaping the battleground of life and seeking another realm, a better or more peaceful one like nirvana or maybe Heaven. What are we trying to get away from? Getting high is getting out of here!

Prayer is running to Source and not away. We pray for answers to big questions: why are we here and what is our purpose? We ascend to the lap of peace. In honoring World Peace and Prayer Day, we finally stop! We pray, go inner, take a breath, pass the peace pipe, and envision the end of conflict and wars. We take stock; we stop the pollution of our planet and our minds. We change from anger to acceptance, from blame and discord to release. We stop hating and give up the addictions, bullying, or judging others and ourselves. When we STOP we pray! We go within. Look at a flower, a face; just look, no thoughts; just take IN whatever is before us. Let it be; stop thinking so that we can hear the gentle words of wisdom. It is said that the memory of God comes to the quiet mind. Let it be, all of it.

Judgment is a lesson we learn early in life, but now we must unlearn it.. Judgment, good or bad, separates us. Throughout history, there has been war and conflict. The name of the road leading to Howard prairie is

Dead Indian Memorial Road. Let's change it. We need to pass the peace pipe around Washington DC and to every country and continent, not to mention all areas of conflict. Our personal and national policy should be "What about the other guy?"

At Native American gatherings, the singing and the drum lead us to the depths of the soul of humankind and allows the yearning we all share to be released to the outer reaches of the universe. Sitting in prayer is acknowledging the Creator and Presence, regardless of culture, social status, race, age, religion, or sexual identity. Joining in prayer, we experience communion, the connection to ALL living things and ALL people. In uniting in the Mind of the Creator, we exclude no one from the circle, the hoop of humanity. There can be nothing better on planet Earth than spreading peace. We are above the fray, above the battleground. We are One. What else could we want?

Red Earth Descendants founder and event host Dan Wahpepah says: "It would be good to walk our lives as a prayer for our future generations, as we believe that is what it truly is. To walk gently on our Mother for the sake of our grandchildren is our responsibility. Let us recognize the truth of this and do our part....If you are doing work for the continuation of all life, this is the place to come." The event is drug and alcohol free.

> *"I am not the victim of the world I see.*
> *²How can I be the victim of a world that can be*
> *completely undone if I so choose? My chains are*
> *loosened. I can drop them off merely by desiring*
> *to do so. The prison door is open. I can leave simply*
> *by walking out. Nothing holds me in this world.*
> *Only my wish to stay keeps me a prisoner.*
> *I would give up my insane wishes and walk into*
> *the sunlight at last."* A Course In Miracles W-57.1:1-9

Painting Watercolor Title: Dancing Indians (From a dream while reading "Black Elk Speaks" in Oregon woods) Prints available: <u>www. sally-mckirgan.pixels.com</u>

Honoring Black Elk - Lakota Medicine Man

Sixty foot faces carved from a broken treaty:
Washington, Jefferson, Roosevelt, Lincoln
Trapped in Black Hills granite Paralyzed since 1939
Stonily gaze over sacred land.
Mt. Rushmore, South Dakota:
Lakota Tribe's sacred hills
Sculpted while hearts on reservations bleed.

To destroy the enemy: Tear down his temple!
Put up your own.
Black Elk, Lakota Medicine Man
Wounded knee witness, rider with Buffalo Bill Cody
Unsteadily hiking finally stands atop Harney Mountain.
Arms outstretched, tears stream down brown wrinkled
cheeks, anointing presidential heads below
Prays to the Grandfathers for his vision to be true:
Restore the sacred hoop with freedom for all hearts!

Loving gargantuan hands, silently but gently
Release stonily trapped granite faces.
Carefully lowers debris to a forgiving earth.
Four frozen President's grateful for release
return the sacred hills to the people.
One broken treaty mended.

Inspired by: "Black Elk Speaks"
by John G. Neihardt, Poet Laureate. Nebraska

THE PROMISE OF CHRISTMAS

It was recently reported in the news that a gentleman in Philadelphia gave away several thousand dollars in $100 bills to individual people in his community. One of our local TV stations gathers new toys to be distributed to children in our communities. The promise of Christmas and the Holidays is seen and heard with the ringing bell of the Salvation Army volunteer and a genuine "Happy Holidays or Merry Christmas" greeting. Either one works for me. The law of love is this: "What I give my brother is my gift to me." When I give good will, I am holding it in my mind, and thus I also have it.

What makes Christmas the cheeriest of seasons is the symbolism of hope associated with a young babe who, although born into poverty, became an awakened being. Not only was he awakened, but also kind and wise, and he had heavy odds against him. The joyful promise of Christmas is that we too can awaken to the kindness we were born with, and it compels us to let it shine forth and heal the suffering in the world. Some in our world may feel that the odds are stacked against them with war, powerlessness, poverty, and injustice, but light and love hold the promise that will overcome all obstacles and self-limiting beliefs.

We are not exempt from the light and love that is our inheritance. This is why we are all fundamentally the same. We inherited the same spark of love and kindness as did that little babe. Let yours go forth today. Give it to everyone you meet and to those you think about, old friends or enemies from the past, and even to those who have passed.

Today the Middle East, not far from where that small babe was born, has become a humanitarian disaster zone, producing refugees seeking a place at the Inn. Mothers and Fathers with babies and children run from harm's way, asking for shelter and mercy, and many encounter rejection and obstacles such as closed borders or being turned away. The Prime Minister of Germany, Angela Merkel, has become the voice of reason and compassion. She is like a Harriet Tubman, holding the light in the darkness of mistrust and loathing. There are some in our country who are distrustful of refugees, but we cannot let fear stand in the way of tolerance, good will and compassion. We may be at war with terrorism, but surely we are not at war with families with children. I recently wrote a hypothetical letter to ISIS. Since the mystics tell us we share the same Mind, perhaps the message will reach some crevice of grey matter somewhere in time. I share it below. You may not agree, and I invite you to write a letter from your heart.

Dear ISIS and Supporters: I understand your hate and your misery. Everyone, if they are truthful, recognizes the hate they harbor in their heart at times. Hate damages the soul. Many in the world hate you too. I am sorry for hatred and pain, but know that this need not be. Hate is a choice. You are in charge of what you think about others. Allah is love and so are you. No one is without the spark of love they were born with. You may hate me, but what you think of me does not determine what I think of you. I choose to exclude no one from my love. It gives me peace to be inclusive. Jesus said, "Love your enemies," and Mohammad said, "Do not get angry" (www.islamawareness.net). This may sound simplistic, but let's bring our favorite food to the table and talk it out. Afterwards, we will sing songs of peace to each other! May Allah/God guide all faiths and non-believers to the path of peace and brotherhood so that the entire Family of man will know its Oneness and live in Peace and Good Will forevermore.

> *"You can wait, delay, paralyze yourself, or reduce your*
> *Creativity almost to nothing. But you cannot abolish it.*
> *You can destroy your medium of communication,*
> *but not your potential. You did not create yourself."*
> A Course In Miracles T-1.V.1:5-8

COLUMNS 2014

SURRENDERING TO THE INEVITABLE

"When something has gone to the trouble of happening, it is best to consider it inevitable, in my opinion." Movie: "My Talks with Dean Spanley," with Peter O'Toole and Sam Neil

Sometimes while reading a book or watching a movie, a statement will jump out and you can't write it down fast enough. The above statement was a beautiful reminder of how we "suffer" when we cannot accept what evidently was inevitable. When something tragic happens, we experience horror and non-acceptance immediately: "Oh My God, I don't believe it." It is a total shock. Unless we can come to accept that it was somehow inevitable, it will continue to traumatize us for months, years, and decades in a never-ending stream of past memories.

In the past year we had an unexpected sudden death in our family. We wonder "Why him?" Or "Why us?" Our emotions fixate, and we are consumed by the "If only ___" or "What if ____" or "Why didn't ___" and the rollercoaster of regrets. However, these thoughts are a waste of psychic energy if it was inevitable in the first place. It was supposed to happen, and so it did; it was preordained, so let it go.

Mystics and spiritual teachers say this world and everything in it is an illusion and that life is a classroom. Each soul comes to learn lessons for its progression, and everything that happens is part of the "script" for that soul's lesson plan. Dr. Brian L. Weiss in his book, "Many lives, Many Masters," recounts several startling cases of past life regressions with case histories of soul evolution through reincarnation. If our true identity is Spirit, eternal, changeless, and formless, then no one dies or even can die. Bodies die, however, and we believe the body is "who" we/ they are and become attached to them; we love them. When we realize the eternal Spirit residing within each of us is our identity, we will not suffer when inevitably the soul/spirit leaves the body that hosted it. We each have an individual script and lessons to learn, but our Spirit/Soul never dies.

Whatever our script may be, we have two choices: to listen to the voice of love within our mind or to the ego voice of fear. The ego thoughts, "regret, if only, or why," will keep the misery, guilt, blame, grief, and emotional distractions going forever. How long do you want to suffer? Vigilance is needed because thoughts are seemingly as innocent as a fuzzy drifting dandelion seed until they land and take root. Here's an exercise: Simply watch all thoughts of regret and pain; do not judge yourself; don't deny or believe them; just notice and observe the ego in action. Then withdraw your belief in them. Wait for peace to descend. When you feel peaceful again, say:

> "I can be hurt by nothing but my thoughts.
> The Thoughts I think with You can only bless.
> The Thoughts I think with You alone are true."
> A Course In Miracles W pll- 281.1:5-7)

By holding the hand of love within your mind, the ego thoughts are seen for what they are. You, the director of your powerful mind, can change them by choosing Love within. Looking and letting go of regret and ego-held grievances is true forgiveness. Accepting is surrendering; it was a lesson for all the souls involved. It was inevitable and nothing could have been done differently, because it wasn't! We give up blame and all residue of resentment. We always share the Love and Oneness with those who have gone. The mercy of inner peace is now present.

SAY IT WITH LOVE

Can you think of a time when you wish you had said something differently or had not said what you did? We all have. But think of what might have been said if love was held in the mind. Perhaps you were angry at the time, but if we can remember to stop before we say something, take a breath and access the place within where love resides, we can trust what we will say will be loving. We don't know what the words will be, but we can trust they will come from compassion, our true identity, the higher self, the wisdom shared with the Creator/God/Allah/Yahweh/Holy Spirit/Jesus, i.e., Love. The other will recognize the love being offered and will not be offended.

There is a place in you where peace and stillness abide. It is found only within and nowhere outside or in the world. The world can serve as a reminder of the sacred place, and we visit cathedrals, holy places, and perhaps nature in search of peace, but while being beautiful, these things are merely echoes of what was first held in the mind.

Nourish, practice, develop, and cultivate this center, the spirit Self that you are. It is the place to go when chaos arises, where the wisdom of love resides, and where to turn and ask, "What would you have me say?" Be aware, it is the ego part of the mind which usually speaks first. The ego mimics love, but the difference is it's manipulating rather than peace making.

The more you practice finding that "still center," the faster you will become at accessing it. The feeling we have when something is amiss sends us into fear or love. We usually go to fear, but the instant you realize you are feeling fearful or upset, and it is not what you want, go to that place of refuge. Say, "I'm feeling upset but I now choose the love within to guide me." There are many spiritual paths that can help, but the only one who can do it is you. There is a beautiful old hymn: "*You gotta walk that lonesome valley, you gotta walk it by yourself; nobody else can walk it for you. You gotta walk it by yourself.*" We all walk the lonesome valley, but help is within yourself, in your powerful mind.

Eckhart Tolle's book, "A New Earth," has a chapter called "Recognizing Inner Space." We have so many thoughts and distractions in the world that we are not aware of the consciousness of our true Self within. If we listen to our thoughts of worry, despair, achievement, anxiety, and negativity, we will not enjoy the simple things like watching clouds, the rain, and the flash of a blue jay or sunlight on a flower. He goes on to say "Stillness is the language God speaks and everything else is a bad translation." As we become mindful, we realize we can access this quiet space anytime, even while sitting through a tough meeting or watching a disaster on TV. Tolle says a space has opened in the mind, no matter how briefly, in the otherwise incessant stream of thinking. As we nurture and develop the inner center, let our awareness see and hear beauty; we expand the spacious place of love in the Mind.

Choose to be and speak from that center of love that you are. When you go to the still place, remind yourself: "I choose the love that is at my center to guide me. I ask to be guided by love." Ask for help. You don't know what you will say, but you can trust it will be something kind, loving, and helpful. And don't worry if nothing seems to come at that particular moment, but trust that when the time is right you will say it with love, the love that you are, coming from the stillness within! Ask for HELP! The intuition, guidance and help will come. Stay open.

Painting Watercolor Title: Help!! – Watercolor –
Available at: www.Sally-mckirgan.pixels.com

GRADUATION ADVICE TO MY KINDERGARTENER

My grandson is graduating from pre-school and will even wear a cap and gown! Here's some advice for him to remember as he negotiates kindergarten, grade school, and beyond, to the coming inevitable lessons.

You have a light, a spark within that is your true identity. Everyone has it. It connects us to God whether we realize it or not. This light is your Soul/Spirit, your gift from God, and it is why you are the light of the world. It is in everyone—no exceptions. Connect to it every day, for it gives energy in the form of Love! See the light in others. Sometimes if you forget, the light in others will inspire you. Knowing this light is "being in spirit." It connects to love and is always merciful and accepting.

You have two types of thoughts that run through your mind. One speaks of kindness and acceptance. The other speaks of fear and judgment. They are exact opposites. You have a powerful mind that can decide which one to follow. One voice speaks of love and will make you happy. The other, the ego, will make you feel alone and separate. Follow the kind voice even if you think it will not make you popular or rich. It is from the wise Spirit within, i.e., intuition, an inner feeling or knowing. It knows the peaceful way. Follow its advice.

You can choose peace when things are chaotic around you by saying: *"I am spirit, the light of the world. I am Loved."* Breathe in and say it over and over. You are pouring "calm" onto the mind's chaos and remembering your true identity is spirit and not ego. Quietly listen, because truth within has something important to tell you. God is pure LOVE and never condemns.

When you are afraid or think people do not like you, or if they bully you, tell them with your thoughts: *"You are the light of the world along with me,"* and smile at them. Make a friend. Invite them over. When you reach out, they may say "no," but deep down they want to say "YES." The important thing is that you have said "yes" to them. When we help others, we help ourselves as well. See things as either love or a call for love.

Be honest if you find yourself disliking someone there is something in yourself you dislike. Ask yourself "What is it that bothers me?" Maybe you wish you were like them, as smart, rich, talented, or had their toys. Your ego thoughts are creating judgment and separation. Don't believe them but look at them and say: *"I have everything because I am loved by God and so are they."* Bless them for their gifts, and know they are loved as you are. This is how to forgive and let go.

When you give, you receive. You can give things away and they are no longer yours. But when you give love away with your thoughts, it returns because love is in your mind. If you give fear, it also returns because it is in your mind. Which feels the best?

This all sums up to this: Be kind no matter what comes or may happen. Everyone has problems in life, everyone has fears and worries that they do not talk about. Let kindness for all including yourself guide you in life. You can stand up for yourself but do so from the love within. Bring the gifts you were given at birth, and share them with the world. Exclude no one from your love. Not even a murderer. He/she has suffered and did not know they were loved. Give compassion and have compassion. Give hate and you have hate within.

Congratulations! There may be more advice in the years ahead, but for now remember to love yourself, everyone you meet, and have fun.

> *"Only God's holy children are worthy channels of*
> *His Beautiful joy, because only they are beautiful*
> *enough to hold it by sharing it. It is impossible for*
> *a child of God to love his neighbor except as himself.*
> *That is why the healer's prayer is:*
> *Let me know this brother as I know myself."*
> A Course In Miracles T-5.in.3:5-8

CASE DISMISSED: THERE GOES THE JUDGE!

I recently had a dream in which I was standing before a stern-looking Judge. He looked grim, with a black robe and white frizzy hair. I was frightened. Then his gavel came down hard and loud, and he shouted "Case dismissed" and smiled! Wow—the relief was wonderful.

Maybe it was my subconscious alerting me to the judgments I make about others. It is so easy to look at someone and put them in a box and decide who they are and what they are about.

We are born sitting on the "bench," with a gavel in our chubby fist making judgments about others for the rest of our lives. We are taught by well-meaning parents to be careful of some types of people or perhaps of a hot stove. After all, our entire world is not a safe place; it's not Heaven. We grow up judging this one and that one. But after adulthood, why do we keep it up? The ego mind, set on automatic, continues to separate, divide, and fragment into social groups, religions, and ethnicities, with diverse political views and on and on. We divide and separate like cells run amok until we find ourselves in tight and constrictive boxes where we can hardly breathe, experiencing no freedom and certainly no happiness. We were trained well, but we end up exclusive rather than inclusive, and in exile, afraid and lonely. We long for and are seeking something, but what? I think it is the expansiveness of a calm and free uncluttered mind.

It is possible to unclutter the mind. When we've finally had enough of the world's distraction and confusion, we can choose to cease being a puppet of the ego's thoughts. We become a decision maker who can choose what and how to think about something or someone. We can make new choices, meaning we can change our mind. We are no longer gullible or in lockstep with the ego's stream of endless thoughts. It is in realizing we hold the key to changing our thoughts that we step off the wheel of the monkey mind and attain inner peace. It entails vigilance and watching the ego with an eye of detached observation. We wake up more and more as we become aware of how the mind works.

Stepping down from the judge's bench, we step up to the observation deck. We become aware of how the judgmental thoughts make us feel: fearful or peaceful? Choosing peace is being good to yourself. Embracing fear is an un-kindness. We need to honestly look at our fears and see if they are based in reality. But mainly, they are just automatic responses from our conditioning. Loving thoughts heal because love is the healer in our mind. We are on the road to health and liberty when we refuse to believe every judgmental thought that comes along. Observe and just let go. In letting go, we are forgiving! What was the thought for? Attack is for separation. We don't love what we attack because we have already condemned it.

When we look at our lives and the world, we can see the pain judgment causes, i.e., the division and disagreements. Watching a TV news program, you can see how disconnected we are from each other. I've noticed that many news programs now have a short "human interest" story. Why? To offset the negative separation they have been reporting.

What a relief it is to give up judgment. We can live safe and healthy lives and even disagree with someone, while still holding kindness in our mind. We have just gone through an election, and even if we do not agree with each other, we are still One people, community, and human family. In kindness and compassion, all disagreements and judgments dissolve because we understand that underneath the ego we are the same. Case dismissed!

A Scaredy Snake?

Afraid of snakes that slither near?
One day I met one full of fear!
I observed: Mr. Snake,
ancient fears gone: I felt clear, awake!
I slowed my pace, he stopped on a dime.
He was the fearful one this time!
Looking for a second we both starred.
Why did he seem so very scared?
He quickly darted whence he came.
Do you think he feels blame?
For that garden stunt, bringing Eve such shame?
Poor snake feeling guilty and in such fear!
Choose forgiveness! Now! And all will be clear!.

COLUMNS 2013

CELEBRATE EASTER: CHOOSE PEACE

"Very little is needed to make a happy life; it is all within yourself, in your way of thinking." Marcus Aurelius

"Economic factors, personal psychology, impulsiveness, aggressiveness, pleasure, i.e., Utopia, will fail because people have their hate, their need to be loved, and special interests." Quote attributed to Sigmund Freud

Marcus Aurelius, Roman Emperor from 161 to 180, is considered an important Stoic philosopher. His Stoic tome, Meditations, written in Greek, described how to find and preserve equanimity in the midst of conflict by following nature as a source of guidance and inspiration.

Freud, 1856 to 1939, was intrigued by the equanimity proposed by Marxism, but he finally recognized that if we don't deal with the ego (unconscious of the psyche), no form of government would ever work, whether Communism, Socialism, Despotism, or Capitalism, because they all contain the aggression of the ego. The ego seeks an enemy, someone to hate or disagree with, i.e., the scapegoat. Because of the ego nothing will ever change in the world. As a result, the world has had nothing but wars since the beginning. We continue to disagree and find someone, a country, a culture, a race, a religion, or person to hate. Attack always follows. Following the ego's attack is guilt, and then we are trapped. But just because nothing will change in the world does not mean that we cannot change our minds, thoughts, and lives. As Marcus Aurelius said, the solution is "within yourself, in your way of thinking."

We can have peace if we decide to be 100% responsible for the WAY we understand what we see. And what do we know really? We always LOOK outside and never within. The Course In Miracles, a non-dual combination of Philosophy, psychology, and spirituality, prods us in lesson 34: "I could see peace instead of this." We can see things either as an attack or a call to choose peace. If we see attack, the ego is feeling threatened and needs to retaliate, to do something. Humanity is over 7 billion worldwide, and even when from the same city or state we do not agree! But we do not have to attack just because we disagree. We have a split mind, and the way you feel will tell you if you are using the ego or the right mind of peace. We can disagree with kindness, and that is choosing peace instead of attack. When you dislike someone, look within at the judgments. Where do they come from? Old beliefs or your own projections you prefer not to accept? The ego mind feeds on disagreement and separation and always looks for differences. Peace sees everyone as equal. We see the split mind clearly in Aurelius' "way of thinking" and Freud's "hate, needs, and special interests."

Here are some suggestions in choosing which mind or thoughts to listen to. Take a few minutes each day and watch your thoughts. You will see the busy ego mind, but DO NOT judge, just watch, observe objectively, and become aware of the chatter. Who is watching the thoughts? YOU ARE the stillness behind the thoughts. That stillness, in the right mind, is the stately calm within; it is who you are as Spirit, as Love. If you have a thought that you would NOT share with everyone—it is not from the right mind of Spirit.

When you have an impulse to do something…wait. The impulse will pass. The ego mind always speaks first. Then let the Love in your right mind guide you, and you will do the right thing in every situation, and there will be no guilt!

Be the joy you want to see in your world. Smile and you will be smiled upon. And you never know, but your smile could have a profound effect on someone who is suffering, silently. Exclude no one from your Love. Love never compares or condemns, and it brings equanimity to all. Enjoy spring, nature is awakening around us! Celebrate Easter and the end of death. Resolve to live in your loving and kind right mind, and gradually the ego will diminish. Choosing the peace within makes us happy.

> *"There is no death because what God created shares His life.*
> *There is no death because an opposite to God does not exist.*
> *There is no death because the Father and the Son are one."*
> A Course In Miracles W p1 - 167.1:5-7

THE INNER PEACE DIPLOMA

Hurrah! Graduation time! What a thrill for graduates, their families, and friends to see dreams accomplished. We know life is a process of gains and losses; everything changes and nothing is ever certain in this world, but how we respond will determine our happiness and that will affect society. Will they graduate knowing how to attain inner peace in this unpredictable world?

His Holiness, The Dalai Lama, speaking at the University of Oregon on May 10, 2013 said: *"Peace must come through inner peace. First inner peace starts from each individual and not society. We change society when each one makes an attempt to change themselves—then society changes. The Individual is most important. Individual freedom is important. Society must change to a peaceful society. Can Self-centeredness be overcome? The practice of altruism and helping others makes one happy."*

He asked educators to help saying, "The education system is very much oriented about the material world—not sufficient. Now today we can shift our responsibility to global warming and warm heartedness, more inner values and care for others well-being. Pay attention about inner value."

In 2005, author David Foster Wallace, 1962–2008, writer and author of Infinite Jest, gave the commencement address to the graduating class of Kenyon College. He, like the Dalai Lama, challenged the educational system to teach compassion to students. Unfortunately, he suffered from clinical depression, but that makes his speech more poignant because he urges us to look beyond the seeming appearances that our eyes see and judge to realize that everyone is fighting a hard battle. He encouraged understanding and compassion and to cease making critical and harsh judgments of others.

Do schools, colleges, and Universities teach anything that might resemble understanding or kindness? If not, Kindergarten or first grade would be a good place to start and continue throughout the education process. However—Warning! The world might come to a complete STOP! We would stop being selfish; stop bullying and manipulating; stop interfering with other countries; no hatred; political parties might stop arguing; no fearful cultures or strangers to worry about; maybe we would stop buying stuff we don't need; no more projecting our faults onto others or being addicted to news drama on TV 24/7. We might stop suffering and START being kind and love everyone equally like *God does.

What do we gain in feeling separate, lonely, angry, hateful, and fearful? Would we suffer if we saw the spark of eternity in everyone? In Singer/ Songwriter Katy Perry's song Firework, that most teens know, there is a phrase: *"Did you know that there's a spark in you; you just gotta ignite the light and let it shine, just own the night like the 4th of July."* Everyone has the spark, the light. Nothing exists or ever did or still to come that does not have it. Imagine how our society would be if we began projecting or seeing "that spark" and light in everyone. That would be to make a conscious choice to either see their spark or draw the veil of judgment. If we look lovingly on them, they will know that they are part of you and you of them.

Why are we here? What/who am I? Philosophers attempt to answer it, as do Theologians. Thinkers and writers from all ages have grappled with this question. One thing for sure is: We are here. So we can make good use of the time we have and realize our identity, our spark, our inner beauty, our kindness, and know we always try to do our best and forgive ourselves when we don't. The bottom line: we all want to know we are loved and that we are forgiven. That's graduation with inner peace.

*God. A Love not of this world, but love's reflections seen here are: kindness; mercy; all-encompassing equality; Oneness. No one is excluded. Ever!

> *"We have begun the journey. Long ago the end was*
> *written in the stars and set into the Heavens with*
> *a shining Ray that held it safe within eternity and*
> *through all time as well. And holds it still;*
> *unchanged, unchanging and unchangeable."*
> A Course In Miracles, C. ep. 2:4-6

THE LIGHT OF FORGIVENESS

You are the light of the world! Light is stronger than darkness because it extinguishes it. Can the sun be extinguished? Clouds can cover it and make it obscure, but it still shines. The light within you cannot be extinguished. It can be covered over, but it is still there. It awaits your recognition and acceptance. This is not a statement of pride, arrogance, or self-deception. You have not thought of yourself as light because you have been taught otherwise, but you can learn the truth about your true identity.

We have a split mind. One part of the mind gets upset and feels like a victim. The other part contains the "light and love" of your Spirit. If you feel upset, it is the ego, the false self you are listening to and have mis-identified with. You are NOT your ego. Everyone makes an ego for him/herself, and the ego convinces us that the body is who we are. We obsess over the body; we dress it, feed it, wash it, have its needs met, take it to the doctor or dentist and to concerts or plays to make it happy, and then we drug it with aspirin, Tylenol, or various drugs or alcohol. In this world of form, our identification is taken over by the ego, and it keeps the distractions going so that we will never awaken. It does not want you to know that you have a mind and a light within that cannot be extinguished or damaged. Of course, we take care of the body because it is our learning device, but at some level we know the body/ego is not who we are.

What would you see in the world? The choice is yours, but learn and do If someone cuts you off in traffic, do you lose your peace? If you are angry and feel defensive, you have lost your peace and are in the ego's corner. Ask yourself if it is worth getting upset about. Do you like the feeling of being a victim or a martyr? Sometimes we do. When someone says something upsetting, just imagine whatever was said as bouncing off your light. Just smile! See it as either love or a call for love. Go within and ask your light/spirit/self if there is something to say or do? If there is, it will come from love, and maybe you'll send flowers. Holding onto grievances only hurts you.

For inner peace, look at the ego but withdraw from its advice or directives. Little by little, as you choose to recognize the light within, the less ego thoughts and more beautiful moments of peace will be yours. The ego is nothing more than a thought, a belief. Don't associate with its fear and it will vanish. You can be hurt by nothing but your thoughts. The thoughts we have under the ego's direction cause pain and separation. Who is in charge of running these thoughts? You have an inner decision maker that chooses which voice to hear.

not let your mind forget the law of seeing: You will look upon that which you feel within. If fear is within your heart, you will perceive a fearful world; if envy is in your heart, you will be envious; if love is in your heart, you will look out upon a world of love through the light of forgiveness.

You are Light and nothing sticks to light. Train your mind and say: "Forgiveness is my function as the light of the world." Listen to love and laugh at the ego. Be like Teflon—everything brushes off easily—forgiveness does likewise. The light in you forgives everyone and everything. What could life's problems and lessons be for if not for the light of the world's forgiveness? Forgiveness is a gift you give yourself by remembering your identity as the light of the world.

> *"There is a light in you which cannot die; whose presence*
> *is so holy that the world is sanctified because of you.*
> *All things that live bring gifts to you, and offer them in*
> *gratitude and gladness at your feet. The scent of flowers*
> *is their gift to you. The waves bow down before you,*
> *and the trees extend their arms o shield you from the*
> *heat, and lay their leaves before you on the ground that*
> *you may walk in softness, while the wind sinks to a*
> *whisper round your holy head."*
> A Course In Miracles W p1 -156.4:1-4

Painting Watercolor Title: One Family, One Planet, One People -
Arising from the Divine all religions arose from the same Source. Sally-
McKirgan.pixels.com

INTERNATIONAL PEACE DAY
& INTERNAL PEACE DAY

Holding on to anger is like grasping a hot coal with the intent of throwing it at someone else; You are the one who gets burned. Quote attributed to The Buddha

The UN declared September 21 as International Day of Peace thirty-two years ago. Now, near the beginning of the 21st Century, why not declare an "Internal" peace day, and encourage the people of world to look at the "hot coal" dwelling within.

The problem: Everyone has an ego, the "hot coal" that when unchecked governs their life. The solution: Everyone has a decision-making mind that can regulate that "hot coal and dissolve it and obtain internal peace.

Mindfulness vs. mindlessness means looking at that "hot coal" throughout the day. We watch the antics of the thoughts running the show and making decisions. As we watch the drama, the projections and the judgments we observe, we look. If looking, we are no longer in denial: "There's that anger again." Look and DO NOT JUDGE; see the thoughts; let them go. What we focus on grows! The ego has grievances, grudges, judgments, jealousy, and strategies to manipulate in order to get its way, while thriving on guilt and fear. Don't believe it.

You have a powerful mind! You have power in looking, watching, and, most importantly, letting the ego thoughts go. Refrain from judging the stream of concerns, worries, resentments, and judgments. Your power is in replacing them with the sanity within. Ask: "Does this thought bring me internal peace?" And "Do I want to see this differently?" You are the decider, a powerful decision maker who can both believe and follow the insanity of the ego or the sanity of the love within. By watching the ego, it is gradually undone and becomes less and less dominant. You will notice when you are more peaceful!

I overheard a conversation about "those Muslims." One was holding a grudge about the attack on the World Trade Center twelve years ago. The memory was making him miserable and he was projecting hate on all Muslims, holding onto the grievance. Sometimes we enjoy our grievances. If he would become mindful and watch his thoughts and realize how he felt, he would see what he was doing to himself. The hate hurts only the self! Every time he reads or sees what he thinks is a Muslim, he gets another "hit," which builds up the pain. If he said "I want peace instead of this," he would have it! He could also imagine himself walking into a Mosque, being greeted with "As-salam alaykum" (peace be upon you), and shaking hands with the Imam and experiencing peace being in the Mosque.

You are not your ego, and it is not your friend. You are mind, the higher self, Spirit loving and lovable, an innocent Child of God. You have done nothing wrong. Case Dismissed! No longer identified with the ego, you listen to the quiet truth whispered softly coming from the One loving mind we share with everyone. You are as God created you, a spark of eternal spirit, changeless, formless, and loved. You are One with God, like a baby in the womb, resting peacefully in Oneness. You are having a dream of the world, your life, its trials and successes, but you can awaken in time, right now, and claim your true grandeur and identity as Spirit. No longer living as the ego's chattel, your internal peace reflects a life at peace, inspiring others, your community, and sends echoes of peace around this war-weary world.

> *"As the ego would limit your perception of your Brothers to the body, so would the Holy Spirit release your vision and let you see the Great Rays shining from them, so unlimited that they reach to God."*
> A Course In Miracles T -15.IX 1

LOVE DOES NOT JUDGE

Is it possible to love someone and at the same time judge or condemn them for something? Maybe they are not doing what you would do or have asked, e.g., teens getting home late, quarreling with your partner over spending or not spending on the right things, children or grandchildren acting out and annoying you. These are irritations in our lives, but WHO is annoyed? Identify the part of your mind that is upset. It is the part that is impatient, judgmental, and angry, demanding punishment. Yes, parents need to discipline children, but it can be done with love, calming verses, anger, or blame. The ego mind judges and demands discipline, but it is not your identity. You are much more than that.

The goal of a peaceful life unfolds when we retrain the mind and withdraw belief from the ego's schemes. In doing so, we discover our true identity. It amounts to changing our mind and accepting the love that we are. The ego tries to cover up the love, but you know, at some level, it is there and it is you. We gradually come to recognize that the love has been there all along.

If we listen to the ego's voice, we will never love unconditionally. The ego's way of loving amounts to manipulation to get its way or in giving to get. What's in it for me? Challenge yourself to watch its gyrations and observe it, but don't believe, listen, or follow it. Just look and laugh! Even something as innocent as going to lunch or dinner and seeing someone the ego judges as "different." Maybe it's their annoying clothes, their voice, or the way they chew food. It is an egoic judgment, and it is 100% separation. That person could be someone you have longed to meet (a favorite author or a professor of quantum physics), if you only knew! The ego does not know anything. Judgment separates us into lonely boxes. Even a "good" judgment—for example, "what beautiful hair she has," which really means I do not have hair like that and so we are different and not alike. We have separate bodies and the ego likes to compare. The trump card is you have a Mind that chooses to listen or not to thoughts of separation. And if you judge yourself gently, let the thought go because guilt is an ego trap.

Imagine what it feels like to be deeply accepted, loved, with no stress and calmly guilt free. Feel that within; give it to yourself and you will give it to others. If you condemn, you can also be condemned. Whatever you do to others can and will be used against you. Condemn, and you are a prisoner of guilt; but love, and you are guilt free. We feel guilty when we attack. Love sweeps all ego beliefs away with a gentle hand of compassion.

Believe in your worthiness and disengage from the ego's games of criticism. Love is within and not found out there in the world. Go within and think of someone who has loved you unconditionally. If you cannot identify anyone, then entertain the thought of an all-loving Creator–Yahweh, Allah, Jesus, Mohammed, Krishna, or God (or your dog)—beaming love at you like a laser beam. Feeling it, it is yours. Recognize that it is your inheritance. You are no longer lost. Love found you. Hear the inner voice telling you of your identity: a loving mind choosing love, gives love. Everyone is included in the same identity of Oneness.

Wear that identity into the world. Look at the upsets mentioned earlier with that love. There is a blessed relief that washes over us when we realize our Oneness with everyone and all things. All bitter struggles, the distractions, and loneliness end when we refuse thoughts of separation. Be a love finder, not a fault finder, and pure joy will fill your mind and Peace Prevails.

My Sweet Little One

What if the birds were afraid to fly,
where would we be, you and I?
What if the flowers were afraid to bloom,
to burst forth and brighten your room?
What if the fish were afraid to swim,
floating about scared to dive in?
What if the clouds were afraid to rain,
to moisten your brow and ease the pain?
What if the grass was afraid to grow,
unable to feel the soft wind blow?
What if the sky was afraid to be blue,
to hold the sun to watch over you? Or....
What if God's Love was only for some?
Then be afraid, my sweet little one!

COLUMNS 2012

WHAT KIND OF DAY DO YOU WANT: GRIEVANCES OR FREEDOM?

Letting go of present and past upsets is easy, right? How were your Holidays? Did you pick up new upsets or grievances to add to the collection? Letting go of them is easy, if only we will do it. Why don't we? Someone said the definition of stupidity is doing the same thing over and over and expecting different results. If we continue to think the same thoughts over and over, we will continue to find ourselves mired. But, if we change those thoughts...Hallelujah! Why not become as adept at dropping the offenses and thoughts as we are in acquiring them? Changing our minds is the solution. Like the scarecrow, who didn't have a brain, said to Dorothy, "The best place to start is at the beginning." Many spiritual paths encourage us to begin each day with an affirmation or a positive thought. Each morning upon awakening, ask yourself: "What kind of a day do I want? How do I want to feel no matter what happens to me or someone else?"

You may have heard the story of the two friends who, as they walked to work each day, one of them would stop to buy a newspaper from the same rude vendor. "Why do you buy a paper from him when he is always rude to you?" The friend replied, "I don't give him or anyone the power to take my peace away. How he treats me does not determine how I will treat him."

If we start the day with the intention of not giving our power away by letting incidents upset us, at least we know what we want. We have these invisible buttons on our chest. Some buttons may be more sensitive than others, but remember: you are the one who decides what is sensitive, and you have your finger on the trigger. We call them our "pet peeves." They are our pets because we like them. We like getting upset. We are choosing it. You can list them and rank them from slightly annoying to downright repulsive. You are the judge, and your judgment comes from past experiences. The past is where the buttons were created.

Write down your response to the question "What kind of a day do I want?" and tape it your bathroom mirror. Each morning as you get ready for the day, read your statement to help start the day. Maybe make an extra copy to carry in your pocket or place in other areas, like by the telephone, refrigerator, car, or kitchen counter. As you go through the day, make a point of being aware when you change your thoughts, and remember your intention. If you keep a journal, give yourself a star every time you changed your mind when buttons were pushed. If you reacted, do not beat yourself up. You just made a mistake, that's all. You could even mark an "x" on your bathroom reminder and give your Self credit when you noticed a button reaction but changed your mind. YOU are now gaining control from automatic ego re-active responses and beginning conscious living.

The more you do it, the stronger you will become, and more and more peace will be yours. Yes, buttons will be pushed, but your change of mind and feelings about them will be less intense. The buttons will be noticed, but you have given them the brush-off. That is freedom!

Be kind to yourself when something triggers your memory, when the floodgate holding back resentment opens and emotions and thoughts flow freely. These buttons from the past are still lurking about. How do you feel? Remember, your reminder is in your pocket. Ask yourself: "Do I want to live in the past and give my power away?" A memory from the past can and will take your peace away, but it is up to YOU to stop it. Is the memory helpful? If not, let it rest in peace and you will too. Forgiveness is freedom when you remember it is FOR GIVING your Self the peace you want.

> *"Grievances are completely alien to love.*
> *Grievances attack love and keep its light obscure.*
> *If I hold grievances I am attacking love,*
> *and therefore attacking my Self.*
> *My Self thus becomes alien to me.*
> *I am determined not to attack my Self today,*
> *so that I can remember Who I am."*
> A Course In Miracles, W- 84.3:2-5

THE PEACE OF THE FATHER

Many non-dual spiritual traditions tell us life is an illusion, a dream. A Course In Miracles is a non-dual teaching that says we review a journey that was over long ago. Not only is the journey over, but our true identity, as Spirit, resides at home in Heaven and is One with God. Life in the illusion seems otherwise. Every day we hear about disasters around the world.

The cover of the April 8, 1966, edition of Time magazine asked: **"Is God Dead."** The great philosopher, Nietzsche, quoted in Gay Science, Section 125, tr. Walter Kaufmann: *"God is dead. God remains dead. And we have killed him. How shall we comfort ourselves, the murderers of all murderers? What was holiest and mightiest of all that the world has yet owned has bled to death under our knives: who will wipe this blood off us? What water is there for us to clean ourselves? What festivals of atonement, what sacred games shall we have to invent? Is not the greatness of this deed too great for us? Must we ourselves not become gods simply to appear worthy of it?"* (Quote from Wikipedia)

According to the Course, God is not dead, but we chose not to remain with Him in Heaven. We had a "tiny mad idea" that we could be our own authority, an individual, on our own and not answer to anyone, be God ourselves. We forgot it was our idea and think he is either dead or blame Him for being an absentee Father. As individuals, we project onto God, for doing what we have done. We left, but we still blame him by calling tragedies "an Act of God" or "God's Will." The unconscious guilt that Nietzsche recognized is enormous. We ran away and we are still doing it from moment to moment.

Speaking of fathers, a few weeks ago we celebrated Father's Day. We buy a gift, send a card, and call if our father is still living. Some hold grievances against their father. But earthly Dads are just that: of the earth; they are human; they make mistakes. The Course teaches that the past is gone and it "can hurt you not." However, in holding onto resentment, you hurt yourself. When we choose to forgive, it cracks open the door to inner peace.

We have one thing in common—we want to be loved. It is what we really DO want. A comforting thing to know is that no matter what kind of father you had, you DO have One who is 100 percent loving, compassionate, kind; Who makes no comparisons and loves everyone equally.

Both Alcoholics Anonymous and the Course teach it is up to us to have a relationship with our true Father. In AA, God is mentioned or referred to in seven of the lovely twelve steps. Step No. 2: *"Came to believe that a Power greater than ourselves could restore us to sanity."* And step No. 11: *"Sought through prayer and meditation to improve our conscious contact with God, as we understood Him, praying only for knowledge of His will for us and the power to carry that out."* The Course has 365 daily lesson that include forgiveness, undo the hurtful thoughts of the ego, and lead us gently back to a relationship with God. Lesson 29: *"God is in everything I see"* and lesson 30: *"God is in everything I see because God is in my mind."* A Course In Miracles W p1 – 30 God is not dead, but His memory resides in a part of our Mind that we uncover as we gradually let go of the ego and its distractions.

No one knows what the Mystery of God is, but the Course says, *"We say 'God is' and then we cease to speak, for in that knowledge words are meaningless. God is Father and Source, Creator and First Cause and His Son (all of us) the created effect all joined as One and united in His perfect Love."* The peace of the Father resides in our mind where it can be embraced.

> *"The memory of God comes to the quiet mind.*
> *It cannot come where there is conflict, for a mind at war*
> *against itself remembers not eternal gentleness."*
> A Course In Miracles, T- 23. I. 1:1

Photo – "Courage" A bench at West Point Academy, N.Y. looking over the Hudson River."

THE GIFT OF ADDICTIONS

It may seem strange to look at our problems or addictions as gifts, but they are life's lessons, so consider them gifts and learn something on the journey. Who runs your life? We live in a dualistic world and have a dualistic mind. It contains both aspects of "good" and "bad." Remember the cartoon of Donald Duck with an angel on one shoulder and the devil on the other? He was conflicted over which one to listen to. We knew which one was the voice of Truth or love. Our world reflects dualism in opposites: love and fear, big and small, hot and cold, reward and punishment, etc. We have the power to choose between these two very different thought systems: spirit and love or fear and hate. The fear/hate aspect thoughts are of the ego and it runs the world. That sounds strong, but the DNA of the ego is attack. The proof is the ceaseless wars since the beginning of existence. We are not civilized. We attack others and declare war. We attack ourselves through addictions. The result is always guilt and anger.

What we learn on our life journey is that the ego is not our friend. It is not our identity or our Truth either. Its only power is given to it when we listen to it and follow it or believe it. By taking charge of the Mind, we take the ego's power away. This is the wisdom of many psychological and spiritual practices, such as Buddhism, A Course In Miracles, or AA, to name a few. The ego cannot change or affect the peace of love within you. For example, the ego mind tells us we have done something wrong. We over indulged, smoked a cigarette, snapped at a friend, or _____ (fill in the blank). We feel guilty. Guilt is the trap. We go around smiling, but deep down we feel terrible thinking, "if they only knew." Feeling guilty is the ego's ace in the hole! "Trapped, trapped like rats," said the cowardly lion in The Wizard of OZ.

Here is a check list the next time you feel trapped and want to STOP the guilt:

1. Go to the Stately Calm Within. As soon as you realize you are suffering and your mind is going around in a maze, STOP. Focus on the breath, center, and stop thinking.

2. Imagine holding the hand of Love. Unconditional, all-knowing, eternal LOVE, whatever that represents for you: Presence; God; Jesus; Allah; Spirit; or Buddha. You can think "Love" no matter what you are doing.

3. Tell LOVE what is in your heart "Love, I really wanted that chocolate cake or _____." Tell LOVE everything, and be honest: "I was depressed because I didn't get that job or he hurt my feelings, or_____."

4. You have looked squarely into your Beautiful Mind and the holy spark you inherited from Love and you've left the ego sucking its thumb. It will come up with plenty of negative chatter. Thoughts from love will always speak of peace. Perhaps you will make amends to someone. Ask Love within to guide you. A thought of condemnation about yourself or anyone is the ego speaking of guilt. Let the ego judgment go. It is not True and you are still LOVE.

5. Now laugh! Start with a phony laugh—"heh, har, ha, hah, ho, ho"—and soon you will really be laughing. This takes the seriousness out of the ego's sails.

If you "slip up" and get mad, it is the ego keeping you in guilt. Repeat the above steps. Looking honestly at yourself is a practice of forgiveness. "Forgiveness is still and does nothing. It merely looks and waits and judges not" (Miracles Workbook pg. 401).

This is Mind training, and you are in charge. That is why it is a gift. You get your Mind back without the ego. We all have addictions or problems in this world. Gradually you take control. You are in charge when you remember LOVE is who you are. Case Dismissed. You are loved, healed, whole, and innocent!

"*The closer you come to the foundation of the ego's thought system, the darker and more obscure becomes the way. Yet even the little spark in your mind is enough to lighten it. Bring this light fearlessly with you, and bravely hold it up to the foundation of the ego's thought system. Be willing to judge it with perfect honesty. Open the dark cornerstone of terror on which it rests, and bring it out into the light.*"
A Course In Miracles T-11.in.3:5-9

GOLDEN KEY TO INNER PEACE

Dr. Emmet Fox, 1886–1951, was a minister, author, teacher, healer, a Christian mystic, and a leader in the New Thought movement. He is known for "The Sermon on the Mount" and "Power Through Constructive Thinking" and more. His lectures in New York, at the Hippodrome, the Manhattan Opera House, and Carnegie Hall were attended by thousands of people. His simple message: *We set our own destiny by our thoughts, words and actions; there is only one presence and power in the universe: God. All else is illusion.* (Source, Wikipedia). A friend recently reminded me of his short booklet The Golden Key to Prayer. It could be called the Golden Key to inner peace because it is a very precise tool to use to stop the inner worry that can ruin a good day. It's about 1200 words and a very easy read. For those with computers, it is available on the web. Following are some of the pertinent points and quotes are from the Golden Key.

He states, that his Golden Key to prayer is a practical recipe for getting out of trouble. "Study and research are well in their own time and place, but no amount of either will get you out of a concrete difficulty. Nothing but practical work in your own consciousness will do that. The mistake made by many people, when things go wrong, is to skim through book after book, without getting anywhere. Read The Golden Key several times. Do exactly what it says, and if you are persistent enough, you will overcome any difficulty."

He continues, *"Prayer will enable you, sooner or later, to get yourself, or anyone else, out of any difficulty on the face of the earth."* And "To those who have no acquaintance with the mightiest power in existence, this may appear to be a rash claim but you need take no one's word for it but simply try it for yourself, and see."

He says that the power to access God "Is not the special prerogative of the Mystic or the Saint, as is so often supposed, or even of the highly trained practitioner. Whoever you are, wherever you may be, it is God who works, and not you, so your particular limitations or weaknesses are of no account in the process." And, you do not have to believe in God, but he asks that you have an open mind and a little faith to try the experiment. Other than that, you may hold any view of God, religion, or none at all.

The method of the prayer is simplicity itself. All that you have to do is: "Stop thinking about the difficulty, whatever it is, and think about God instead. This is the complete rule." He says if you will do this, the trouble, whatever it is, will presently disappear. It makes no difference what kind of trouble it is, small or large. It can be anything, from health, money, jail, law-suit, an upsetting experience, any problem. No matter what it is just stop thinking about it, and think of God instead; that is all you have to do.

The only rule is: "Stop thinking of the trouble and think about God." If you are obsessed on the problem, you are not thinking about God. Do not look over your shoulder to see how matters are progressing or think in advance what the solution could be. That's thinking of the trouble and not God. The object is to eliminate the difficulty and substituting it for the thought of God.

He suggests you choose a simple statement of Absolute Truth to use, like: *"There is no power but God"* or *"God is Love,"* and if it doesn't feel perfect, soon you will find that the "Treatment has begun to take and that your mind is clearing. Each time that you find your attention wandering, just switch it straight back to God." Now that you have the Golden Key, think of God instead of the problem. I find focusing on a problem only makes it bigger; besides, it takes my inner peace and power away!

> *"You first forgive, then pray, and you are healed.*
> *Your prayer has risen up and called to God, Who*
> *hears and answers. You have understood that you*
> *forgive and pray but for yourself. And in this*
> *understanding you are healed. In prayer you*
> *have united with your Source, and understood*
> *that you have never left."*
> A Course In Miracles, S- 3.IV.4:1-5

POLITICAL PEACE—DISAGREE WITH KINDNESS

The season of politics is upon us. Unlike the Holiday Season of "good will to all men," this one can bring out ill will, which is usually directed at whoever is the opposing party! What a funny term, "party," when there is no fun to be had unless everyone is included. At some point, we are all taught to avoid two subjects in polite conversation—politics and religion. We tend to hold strong opinions about them, so to keep the peace we avoid all discussion. It is the polite thing to do. We call the world civilized, but wars are still being fought because of strong attachments and closed minds unwilling to see the other point of view.

We can have inner peace while still disagreeing with others. We can stand up for issues we believe are right and not demean others. It is possible and it takes place in the part of the mind that chooses peace, that part which is your true Self.

I recently attended a spiritual meeting where politics came up, and one brave person confessed to being a member of one particular party. She, as it turned out, was surrounded by members of the other party. It gave everyone pause, and we took stock at the silliness of this division. There we were all dedicated to the larger vision of "Oneness," but it felt as if we were three-year-olds in the sand box.

We soon realized that our "judgments" about having ideological differences is a silly problem. We are friends who think differently. We think differently because of our various backgrounds, culture, education, and so forth. When we stop and hold the other in the "radiant light of truth," that truth trumps all the silly divisions that our ego judgments set up to separate and divide us.

Two thousand years ago, Socrates ran into this very problem. He was using dialog to explore truth. However, it upset those who saw it as an attack on their thought system. They projected "radical or rabble rouser" onto him. He was put to death. Freud's law of projection came into play:

we see aspects, qualities we dislike in someone else and don't stop to recognize we have the same qualities. We project out, onto someone else what we refuse to see in ourselves. Anything deemed intolerable is projected out, and we blame others. We need to turn our pointing figure around and point at ourselves—and then laugh!

A book that eloquently examines how the ego works is Eckhart Tolle's, A New Earth, Awakening to Your Life's Purpose. Regarding holding on to grievances, he says: "If you do (hold on), become aware of the grievance both on the level of thought as well as emotion, be aware of the thoughts that keep it alive, and feel the emotion that is the body's response to those thoughts. Forgiveness happens naturally when you see that it has no purpose other than to strengthen a false sense of self, to keep the ego in place. The seeing is freeing." He goes on to say that honest inquiry is looking at how miserable we feel and choosing not to continue building the ego's false self. Be aware and Present in the Love that is at your core; choose peace and leave the baggage of past thoughts or differences in the dust.

As we go through this political season, remember you are not an ego; you are Spirit, Love, Kindness, and Compassion. Only the ego enjoys attacking and feeling attacked. Our personal power lies in not siding or believing our egoic thoughts. Choose peace instead. It takes practice. It is one of life's major lessons. When you forget and enter the fray and realize you are feeling miserable, just remember to laugh! Laugh and never give up on yourself, your kindness, on peace!

> *Every interpretation you would lay upon a brother*
> *is senseless. Let the Holy Spirit show him to you,*
> *and teach you both his love and his call for love.*
> *Neither his mind nor yours holds*
> *more than these two orders of thought.*
> A Course In Miracles T-14.X.11:4-6

COLUMNS 2011

EVERYONE IS YOUR VALENTINE!

What if everyone was your Valentine? What would that feel like for just one day? Extending love to the cop giving you a ticket; the homeless man asking for bottles and cans; the bank teller; your boss or supervisor; the relative who annoyed you at a Holiday gathering or to whomever or whatever is the target of your latest grievance? Socrates is quoted as saying, "An unexamined life is not worth living." Socrates, the teacher of ethics, fairness, and civility, asked that all conversations occur with respect and without rancor. They had rules back in 350 BCE.

Back to a new age Socrates, Deepak Chopra in the 2002 video God and Buddha, with Robert Thurman of Tibet House, said that when one is in a "mindful" state of love, residing in the heart of creation, it is impossible to hurt or to be hurt. That statement should be engraved on every gun barrel. When we connect with the love in our Higher Self and release the little self, we cease to suffer and cause others to suffer. We suffer only because we do not know who we are. We mis-know ourselves in our struggle with the Universe. The Indian poet Rabindranath Tagore, Asia's first 1913 Nobel Prize winner for Literature, said as he was approaching death, "Death is stalking me every moment; let me accept everything I spurned." What have we spurned in our lives? Do we spurn a particular race, culture, or religion? Do we hold a "grudge" against Arabic speaking people or the Muslim Religion? What are we missing because of that? We miss out on knowing an entire culture with its customs, food, dance, art and, most of all, joining in friendship. We are joyless, separate, afraid, and lonely. Abraham Lincoln said, "To defeat an enemy, make him your friend." We also realize that enmity is not good for our hearts or the immune system. When we forgive we are free and healthier, too. That is called a win-win!

Are we to love only those whom our government says are our friends? We should be free to love everyone and, better yet, get to know them. Look at Vietnam! How many Vietnamese and Americans died? How many men and women today are the walking wounded of war, and suffering or committing suicide because of it? Yet today we are friends with Vietnam.

How wonderful, but did we have to kill and mentally maim thousands to do it? The big question is: Why do we have to go to war before we can become friends?

Chopra tells us we have the natural tendency to be in love with all beings everywhere and be in endless happiness. We are a wonderful machine and nothing in us is separate from the great Self of the Universe. We are One with all. What is stopping us from being happy? We let go of false ego perceptions and judgments. Our natural tendency has been covered up by conditioning, the lies that we believe to be true. When we question our perceptions, we begin to awaken from the sleep of forgetfulness and remember who we are. Buddha means awake. When you awaken, you can still identify with the religion of your choice. Chopra said, "Love is the ultimate truth at the heart of creation. We are all the same being in different disguises. If we peel away the layers of the soul, we begin to go beyond the constricted fabricated self and discover the true self, who we are." There are thousands of paths to walk to "go beyond the fabricated self" and discover the divine being that we are. Visit Deepak Chopra's website at www.deepakchopra.com to see his many books. To name a few: Peace Is the Way; Muhammad; The Ultimate Happiness Prescription; Grow Younger Live Younger; and more.

The benefit of everyone being our Valentine is that we exclude no one and are kind and loving to All. This life is our classroom, our journey to peacefulness and joy. Have a Happy Valentine's Day and Love Everyone! Why not? Just do it!

> *Dream of your brother's kindnesses instead of*
> *dwelling in your dreams on his mistakes.*
> *Select his thoughtfulness to dream about instead*
> *of counting up the hurts he gave."*
> A Course In Miracles, T- 27.VII.15:3-4

My First Best Friend

I'll never forget my very first friend:
Linda was her name.
One happy bright day she appeared,
walking up my sandy lane.
Two bright button blue eyes were
shinning out from a small sweet face.
And two sunny pigtails sticking straight out,
looking for a race.
A baby blue dress tried to cover
her knobby little knees.
The look on her unruffled face:
"I will do just as I please."
She was only five or maybe six
as I was myself.
She had more courage and nerve
than any ordinary elf.
Throughout tall dark woods and salmon
fed creeks summers we would roam.
We built forts, checked chicks in barns
and were never much at home.
One summer night we slept outside
under the milky-way bright.
Ghost stories were read, comics too,
 then we ran around all night
A little scared I was for sure
"What if they found us out?"
My Mom would be mad if she
suspected how we ran about.
She never knew or realized,

I'm very glad to say.
And I wonder what Linda's doing
with her life today?
One time while wandering the woods
a vision I did see.
I told my Mother about it,
but she did not believe
But Linda was ready to go and see
this strange new deal
Off we went into the woods to
learn what the vision revealed.
But to my disappointment,
it was gone and where to, who knows?
But for my best friend Linda,
disappointment made no show.
She must be sailing the oceans,
a fearless adventurer.
Trusting, energetic and never a doubt:
nothing fazed her.
It's been a long time since
I've seen my very first best friend.
But time's an illusion I'm told,
and I know love never ends.
Love is the strongest and mightiest
force on this Earth today
So here's a toast to all best friends,
and for Linda I do pray.

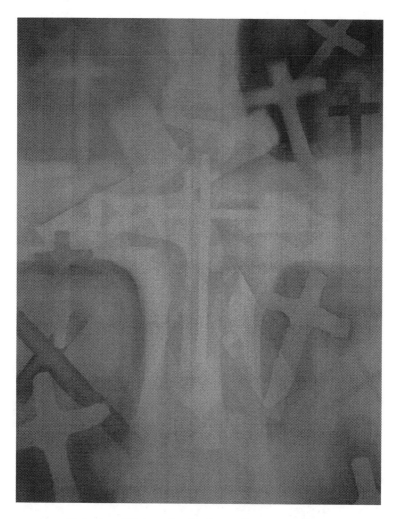

Painting Watercolor Title: Take Jesus off the
Cross Sally-McKirgan.pixels.com

THE FIELD OF NON-JUDGMENT

"Out beyond ideas of right doing and wrong doing, there is a field, I'll meet you there." Rumi, 13th Century Sufi poet and mystic.

We bring so many problems upon ourselves by judging. Why do we continually judge others or ourselves? Let's face it, we like being the judge! We sit on the Judicial "bench" and make one rapid-fire decision after another. "She's too skinny; he's arrogant; they're stuck up; too rich; stupid, homeless, or drug addict?" True, we are taught to discern from our earliest years primarily for our safety by our parents in order to protect ourselves. Watch out for that hot stove, fast cars, biting dogs, steep cliff, stranger-danger, crashing waves, or deep water. Our world is not a safe place; after all, it is not Heaven.

But we grow up, and the fearful monkey mind still is determined to judge this and that. But why do we keep it up? What for? The ego part of our mind continues to use judgment to separate, divide, and fragment ourselves into groups, identified by various religions, nations, ethnicities, political views, societal factions, old; young, rich, poor, and on and on. We divide and separate like cells run amok until we have fit ourselves into a tight and constricting box where we can hardly breathe, and we are certainly not free nor are we happy. We were trained to keep ourselves "safe," but we end up exclusive rather than inclusive and in exile, alone and longing for real friendships, fresh air, and freedom! We also long for the expansiveness of an uncluttered Mind.

We have forgotten that we have a mind with a capital M. When we choose to recognize that our True identity is Mind and Spirit, we cease to be a puppet of the ego and the small m judgmental mind. We remember that we can choose again what and how we will think. We realize we can change our thoughts and get off the wheel of the monkey mind and have inner peace. How? Watch, with detachment, how the small mind works. When we become aware of it, we start to wake up. Becoming the objective observer, you remove yourself from the "bench." However, don't get trapped by judging the small (ego-ick) mind, but rather just look at it and say, "I do not have to believe this thought. It is not true."

We embark on the road to freedom when we refuse to believe every judgmental thought that crosses our mind. Observe it and just let go. In letting go we really are forgiving! You can also ask yourself, "What is this thought for?" Is it a thought FOR separation or FOR joining, for inner peace? Most thoughts are for separation. A thought can be for separation whether negative or positive. For example, "I wish I had her figure" is still a thought of separation because it separates me from her and judges my figure for not being adequate somehow!

We need to take responsibility for what our thoughts create in our lives and the world! When we observe our thoughts, we need to ask: Is this thought for giving Love, unity, and peace, or is it for giving separation and division? If it is for separation, then FORGIVE yourself, GIVE it away, let it go, don't believe it. If it is FOR unity, then realize you are giving Love! We know a thought is loving if we feel peaceful. Peace is all those wonderful combinations of gratitude, appreciation, mercy, compassion, equality, contentment, and, above all, kindness. Loving thoughts heal because we are holding LOVE, the great healer residing in our mind.

What a relief to give up judgment. We may not agree, but once we decide to forgive and choose peace, we are in the field "out beyond ideas of right doing and wrong doing." We are ONE; we are Spirit and Love, where all the disagreements and judgments dissolve and we dwell in the ONE healed Mind.

"The door is not barred, and it is impossible that you
cannot enter the place where God would have you be.
But love yourself with the Love of Christ, for so
does your Father love you. You can refuse to
enter, but you cannot bar the door that Christ holds
open.

A Course In Miracles T-11.IV.6:3-5

WE CAN BE KIND: SEPTEMBER 11, 2011

When we speak up and out for what we believe in, someone always disagrees, but if we will remember to be kind, we will have inner peace. The September 11 families could not agree on whether or not a Muslim Mosque should be built near Ground Zero in New York City. Everyone had their own belief system coming from various life experiences, family, education, culture, time and place, preferences, religious and inbred societal factors of right and wrong, not to mention personal fears. Even these good wounded people, who identified themselves within the same cause, could not agree. Just like Democrats, Republicans, religious organizations, political groups, associations, corporations, choirs, city councils, and non-profits: no one agrees! We come from different perspectives, and we like to hold on to our beliefs, being independent thinkers, but we can have inner peace if we remember to be kind.

The culprit is the ego. We all have one, but it is not WHO we really are. We feel attacked when others do not agree with our thought system, and they feel the same way when we do not agree with them. The key to inner peace: know that your ego will feel attacked and recognize the feeling, but acknowledge that it is the ego feeling this and that YOU can CHOOSE to remember you are not the ego and see the situation differently—i.e., be kind. YOU are the peacemaker within. Your true identity is the peacemaker within, and you are not weakened or discredited because someone does not identify with your thought system. They have come to their belief system just as you have come to yours. We do not need to succumb to the ego's wily ways of separation. Refuse to identify with its beliefs (they are just thoughts), and choose to remain kind and open-minded for inner peace!

Two thousand years ago, Jesus ran into this very problem. He was only speaking truth, as he saw it, yet it upset those who saw it as an attack and threatening to their thought systems. They projected "radical, terrorist, or rabble rouser" onto him. Freud's law of projection came into play: we see aspects or qualities we dislike in others and blame them or attack them rather than recognizing we have the same qualities. We project out upon others what we refuse to see in ourselves. Projection makes perception. It is also called having a scapegoat handy. We just need to turn our pointing finger around and point it at ourselves. It is all false perception. Be kind.

For example, if I oppose a farmer burning slash on his property, what should do? Get a sign and picket the farmer? If inner peace is my spiritual path, I must look within and honestly see whether I have ever done something similar. Have I ever, like the farmer, burned something to get rid of it? Maybe not, but I must look deeper into the issue. Burning something is an easy way to get rid of it, or more simply put: it is an easy way out. When do I take the easy way out to solve a problem? All the time! Now I see that the farmer is no different than I. We both take the easy way out, and I can no longer be angry but, instead, have compassion for him. We are the same; he is trying to solve his problem just like me. Not a bad guy after all.

With the anger replaced by compassion and understanding, I approach him with inner peace as I am seeking to find another way. With that frame of mind, creative opportunities present themselves. When he perceives I am not angry but trying to be part of the solution, his defensive barriers may be lowered. Perhaps not, but having an open mind, being respectful of him, and holding the hand of faith, with kindness as the goal, then we together will find another way. Kindness is a choice.

> *"All your past except its beauty is gone, and nothing is left but a blessing. I have saved all your kindnesses and every loving thought you ever had. I have purified them of the errors that hid their light, and kept them for you in their own perfect radiance. They are beyond destruction and beyond guilt. They came from the Holy Spirit within you, and we know what God creates is eternal."*
> A Course In Miracles T-5.IV.8:2-6

BE THANKFUL LOVE IS YOUR DNA

Can you imagine a world without love? "Love cannot be far behind a grateful heart and thankful mind." That quote from the spiritual psychological book A Course In Miracles, seems to say it all. When we are grateful, we are in Love. When we are appreciative, we hold love in our mind. When we look deeply at anyone or anything with thankfulness, we are in Love. When we hold the "concept" of Love in our mind, many Doctors and Scientists like Deepak Chopra tell us our cells respond. In his book Ageless Body, Timeless Mind, Chopra says that beneath even the most ridged conditioning there is an awareness that accepts the words "I am Love." The reason we can love and be loved is that in the deepest layers of our consciousness there is a knowing that this "love" is where our deepest values are known and where truth is. Love is part of our essential human nature. Chopra goes on to says such words as beauty, compassion, trust, strength, and truth, would be meaningless unless we understood the concept "I am Love" that lies beneath them.

We do not need to be taught how to exist, because being comes naturally. The YOU, the Spirit that comes from love, knows intuitively and does not need lessons in how to love or what to love or why. This Being comes naturally with the nervous system and awareness. Love is considered the most basic emotion that human awareness can feel. Knowledge from primordial feelings in the beginning made us respond to love, trust, and compassion. Love is in our DNA and genetic code and what we seek in life.

As we grow up, we learn the game of social behavior. We forget we are love. We are trained from our earliest years to be nice, polite, and to engage in the game of social behavior. We go along and play the game of pretending to be nice because society (parents) expects it and we do want to be liked. We have to be domesticated and go through this learning process it seems. We play the nice girl or nice boy roles expected of us. But finally, after all this socialization, we come to the point where we want to find out just who or what we are. Are we the roles we play, or is there an authentic self to be found?

When we begin the seeking and search for truth and looking inward for the Higher Self, we uncover the "me" that knows… "I am Love." As we seek to remove the blocks that hide love from our consciousness, we discover what we really are. We start to live from a level of being that remembers "I am Love." We are no longer confused about whether we are lovable, trusting, or valuable because we know we are. Doubts may come and go, but we still know our reality. We no longer have to search for love knowing that it is what we are. We love because we can do nothing else but be the authentic self, with love, compassion, and beauty radiating from our true nature. "I am Love," and it does not matter what I look like or how much money or education I have. "I am Love" whether I am homeless or a zillionaire. I am Love whether I am a prisoner or the warden. "I am Love," but I do not cling to anyone or anything, not even myself. Love is freedom, the freedom to choose my path and to love others as they choose theirs. From A Course in Miracles: "Love which created me is what I am. In peace was I created and in peace do I remain. Now I ask but to be what I am. And can this be denied me when it is forever true?" Be thankful for the Love that we all have within this Thanksgiving.

You are Loved

Do you know you are loved?
Can you feel it in your heart?
Energy from the universe,
surrounded you from the start.
You are bathed in brilliant light
of God's joyful eternity.
It holds you and enfolds you now;
that surely you can see.
There is no need to worry or fear,
about what is ahead.
Because the future is not here,
and you will be gently led.
So let yourself feel the Peace
that is given you forever.
Now you know God Is Love:
He will never leave you, never.

COLUMNS 2010

EXCLUDE NO ONE FROM YOUR LOVE

The truth is that you are loved, loving, and lovable! Accept your reality and extend it to All. That includes your boss, landlord, the US President, Congress or Senate, spouse, partner, annoying relatives, and all perceived problems. Write this down on a piece of paper, and place it where you can see it several times a day:

> I am the Light of the World.
> I am Spirit, Love and Loved.
> Being Love I extend it to all.

Have you noticed that when you give you also receive? When we give donations to a homeless shelter, send money to Haiti, give a dollar to a homeless guy or gal, give time to a Church or favorite charity, spend a few minutes visiting with a hurting friend, tell someone how much we appreciate them, or hold a child or give a smile, we are giving love. And as we give, we receive an inner appreciation in our mind and heart and thus are the recipient of That! When we are kind and loving, the journey, the worldview, or classroom is peaceful and joyful. Since love is eternal, formless, and unending, it cannot run out! You can give away all you want—it will never run out. It is like the magic pot of pudding in the children's story that boils over unceasingly—never to stop! But, love does not make a mess of things; rather, it cleans up messes.

That daily reminder will set the belief in your mind. The ego part of your mind will not believe it, but that does not mean that it's not true. In fact, your ego mind will probably tell you the opposite and deny the reality of what you are. To learn more about the run-amok ego thoughts, there are several books you can read. Here are my favorites: Eckhart Tolle's A New Earth, Awakening to Your Life's Purpose, or Byron Katie's Loving What Is, or A Course In Miracles (365 workbook lessons).

You have the power to change your beliefs and thoughts! Just because you believe something does not mean it is true! We have all made mistakes, have millions of regrets, wonder why we didn't do something we should have and why we didn't listen or hear or learn, and it seems to be a never-ending list that goes on and on. Has this thinking made you happier? When you are in a hole, stop digging! Forgiveness is remembering your true identity as Spirit and Love! You are Spirit having an experience of living in a human body in a classroom called the World. Having an "ego," we all make mistakes. But Spirit is perfection and has done nothing wrong! You are not who you think you are!

Whenever you feel upset, run to that piece of paper you put on your dresser or desk and connect to the unconditional non-judgmental Love within and return to the arms of peace. Many Spiritual Traditions tell us Love is God or God is Love. You do not have to believe in God; just believe in Love. Love Is and You Are Love. Love is a Thought within your mind. Whenever you have a loving thought, you are an extension of Love—i.e., God/Creator/Yahweh/Great Spirit or Allah—and you are the Creator of your life and your world! Let that piece of paper remind you of the limitless love that is within you, and extend it. Because, when you give love, holding it in your mind, it is also yours! Exclude No one from your Love…including yourself!

> *"The Hush of Heaven Holds My Heart Today*
> *Father, how still today! How quietly do all things*
> *fall in place! This is the day that has been chosen as*
> *the time in which I come to understand the lesson*
> *that there is no need that I do anything. In You*
> *is every choice already made. In You has every*
> *conflict been resolved. In You is everything I hope*
> *to find already given me. Your peace is mine.*
> *My heart is quiet, and my mind at rest.*
> *Your Love is Heaven, and Your Love is mine."*
> A Course In Miracles Workbook Lesson W- 286.1:1-9

ARE YOU LOVED? YES!

Who among us feels deeply accepted, loved, forgiven, guilt-free, and the quiet calmness of Presence? Is love possible on this earthly, worldly frame? People come and go; life is ethereal, ever-changing, while aging bodies and political situations—the whims of the ego and duality—toss us about like so much foam on a stormy sea.

Much of my time here on earth I have thought of myself as someone or something separate from everyone and separate from God in particular. After all, what proof is there of Him? What on earth could God have to do with me? Isn't the thought or belief in God just for those who need a crutch? Much of my spiritual seeking was striving for peace but certainly did not including something as elusive as God.

What finally gave me peace was the realization that peace is not possible in duality, which the ego part of our mind rules. However, the ego and duality are not what is True in the final sense. Truth is something that is eternal, unchanging, and therefore real. Nothing in the world is real, because it is not eternal. So when I let the world "go" and see its whims as merely the whims of a restless ego that is never happy, I can finally rest in the knowledge that there is something that is eternal and changeless—and that is where God resides and that is where my true Self also resides. I rest in God. My Spirit/Soul Self, my identity that is eternal, rests there. God is not distant from me. He is separate from my false little ego self but is joined and inseparable from the true larger Self. "I have no life but His." There is a blessing often used in Unity churches that ends with the words "Wherever I am, God is." Yes. My life is God's Life. My true thoughts are God's Thoughts. There is nowhere to go, nothing more to seek. There is nothing to do to find Him; God Is, He is here. He is with me. He is my life. If I live, I am participating in God.

Our only mistake is believing we have some sort of life apart from God. We do not. God is Life. He is Existence. "He is what your life is. Where you are, He is. There is one life. That life you share with Him. Nothing can be apart from Him and live" (A Course In Miracles, Workbook

Lesson 156.2:5). We know bodies die because they are not eternal, but our Spirit, which is part of God, never dies.

And so we go to the quiet place within, where all this is known. We remember daily, "I am as God Created Me," and look past the ego identity. We no longer want to be lost in forgetfulness. We state clearly that we want to leave ego loneliness and find ourselves, as we have always been, at Home. Everyone is included in the Oneness vs. separate ego bodies. And in the quiet, God speaks to us and tells us we are Love and Loved and not shadows of the ego duality we thought we were. We were wrong, that's all—just a silly mistake in our thinking.

There is a blessed relief that washes over us when we realize our unity with God. All the worldly bitter struggles, the fruitless longing, and the aching sense of being on the outside looking in—all of it ends when we let go of the ego and rest in God. A thought of pure joy fills our minds, and Peace Is! At times it bubbles over in compassionate amusement at the tiny mad idea we have tormented ourselves with, that we could ever, in any remote or small way, be separated from Him. Can the sunbeam be separate from the sun? Can an idea be separate from the mind that thinks it? We are an idea in the Mind of God. Peace comes in knowing that Yes! We are Loved and not separate or alone!

Painting Watercolor: Title Daffodil Love Sally-mckirgan.pixels.com

FINDING HAPPY BIRTHDAY PEACE

Are we born only to die? And if so, why? That was my waking thought on the morning of my recent 60-something Birthday! "What a revolting development this is!" I think there was a character on TV who used to say that in disgust. Can it be that we are born, enter the body and the world only to ultimately march steadily and directly to our death? What a (bad) joke!

First, we are born helpless and dependent on others for food and nurturing. We grow up and go to school realizing the time will come when we will need to fend for ourselves and that we need a plan of some sort. Not everyone can figure it out and many become despondent. There are millions of people in prisons who were unable to figure out the system or how to care for themselves.

Here's the kicker—We are all in the same boat living on planet Earth. That is the way the system is, regardless of your ethnicity or Country of origin or your religious affiliation. Everyone, even if you were born with a silver spoon, has to make plans to survive in this world. No one is getting out alive, and everyone is fighting a hard battle!

Who created this world? The ego or God? Would a loving God create a world where we are born only to die? A world where we are born, accumulate knowledge, express our gifts, suffer from an illness or accident, and then die—kaput!—the end? It never made sense to me, regardless of what Church I attended.

I've come to believe this is the ego's world, and it is a "bad joke," and that a loving God could have nothing to do with it. That thought: "God has nothing to do with it" is the cool breeze on the fevered cheek. This is the ego's world, but it is not True and it is not Real. Is there truth in the world? The only reason I am here is to forgive and remember that Love is what I am, and it can be found in my powerful decision-making mind.

The ego does not want us to know we have a mind, period. In coming to this world, the ultimate lesson is to realize, find, and follow the inner wisdom and trust it. The ego will try to keep you from it. That is its job. It offers "seek and do not find" carrots and dilemmas that it insists will make you happy and offers up zillions of distractions. We are all in the same boat whether we hail from Afghanistan to Zimbabwe. Everyone, no matter the lesson that their soul came to learn, has entered a dream, an illusion, and in this world, EVERYONE has the same problem. We think we are separate from God. That is the only problem—our wrong thinking. The good news: It is not true.

In summing this Birthday thought: The ego is a parasite on the mind; it made up a world and bodies that die. If we choose it, which we all did when we came here, it will fill us with doubt, hatred, misery, littleness or grandiosity and throw in a little piece of happiness now and then to keep us going. But it is not True. Only Loving Thought is True. Laugh at the ego, and remember that as you go through your life's lesson, forgive yourself for all your mistakes and those of others, and for coming into this illusion. Dream the best dream you can! Find a spiritual path. If you don't have one, there are thousands, and free yourself from identifying with the World's jailer, the ego. You will then know your invulnerable Spirit Self that never dies and have some Happy Birthday Peace!

My Birthday falls on the 242nd day of the year and the lesson for the day:

> Lesson 242. "This day is God's. It is my gift to Him."
> "I will not lead my life alone today. I do not understand the world, and so to try to lead my life along must be but foolishness. But there is One Who knows all that is best for me. And He is glad to make no choices for me but the ones that lead to God. I give this day to Him, for I would not delay my coming home, and it is He Who knows the way to God."
> A Course In Miracles W.pll – 242

Find out what day of the year your birthday falls on and look up the lesson for that day.

TO HAVE (OR NOT HAVE) HOLIDAY PEACE

Here come the Holidays! We gather with family and friends for a time of sharing and fun and envision something out of a Martha Stewart holiday book, with the festive table, candles burning, and everyone loving, accepting, and happily tolerant. We hope family "issues" are over, and then Aunt Agnes says something. Uncle Charlie takes the "bait," and we feel the quagmire of emotional discomfort cut through the air like a laser through ancient rock. Undercurrents of unresolved emotions erupt. A slight utterance by one becomes the hammer on the head of another. Those who want peace say something to calm the situation, but if that does not work, there are those who will get up, put on coats, and leave while others wring their hands in protest. Sound familiar?

And to be sure, full-blown quarrels don't always ensue, but you can bet resentments and grievances arise and fester away, robbing us of inner peace and contentment, if we let them. That is the point: "if we let them." It is time to take control of how we feel, how we respond, and take our power back! Here are some suggestions. Pick one, two, or all for your Holiday Peace arsenal, and share them with your family.

1. Do not take the bait. If someone says something that bothers you, and you feel your blood pressure rise, recognize that you are being hooked like a fat rainbow trout. Watch your mind carefully. Don't take it personally. Realize what was said was from the "perception" of the other. Just remain quiet, take a deep breath, and do not respond immediately...this is where your power is. We have two inner thought systems built into our mind. One system is the ego. It speaks for attack, revenge, separation, give in order to get, manipulate, etc. The ego responds first (the blood pressure rising) and loves a fight. The other thought system, your higher self, speaks for love and sees everything as either love or a call for love. Your choice: the ego or higher self. For peace, simply go inside and ask your higher

self to respond with love. You will soon know what to say, if anything. Something may surface from the peaceful mind. Responding immediately from the ego will cause guilt for you and the other. The ego's food is guilt.

2. The past is over. How can we see anyone fresh if we continue to impose the past upon them? Memory and judgments from the past keep us and them trapped. Let the past go by dropping your inner "ego" critic, and ask to look with new eyes and vision. Ask to see others differently to let the past go.

3. Watch your projections. The ego part of our mind projects what we dislike about ourselves onto others. Why do you dislike Aunt Rose? Whatever the reason, find it in yourself—maybe not in the exact form, but look for similar content. Example: Aunt Rose seems like a phony; she is never real. When have you acted like a phony? Maybe when you are nervous? Own your projections, but let the ego guilt go. You are not your ego. You and Aunt Rose are both the Light of the World.

4. Forgive and judge not! We forgive when we realize everyone is fighting a hard battle. We, everyone, has made mistakes. So what? Only the ego cares because its food is guilt and blame. Guilt keeps us separate and alone. We really cannot judge because we do not know what our lessons are or anyone else's for that matter. Be compassionate with them and yourself.

In summary: Don't take the bait. Watch the ego mind, and ask your higher self and its loving thought system for help. The past is gone. Watch your projections, and recognize them to let them go. Forgive, and remember that everyone is fighting a hard battle. Be kind to yourself and others for Happy Holiday Peace.

"Let no despair darken the joy of Christmas, for the time of Christ is meaningless apart from joy. Let us join in celebrating peace by The Gift of the Great Rays demanding no sacrifice of anyone, for so you offer me the love I offer you. What can be more joyous than to perceive we are deprived of nothing?"

A Course In Miracles T-15.XI.8:1-3

COLUMNS 2009

HAPPY NEW YEAR: FORGIVE EVERYONE EVERYTHING

Forgive and be free! Forgive them for what they did or didn't do! Exclude no one from the blessing of your forgiveness, including your Self. Forgive your 4th grade teacher, the co-worker who betrayed you, the military, parents, siblings, all relatives, enemies, and friends! And whoever it was who scratched your car without leaving a note. Right now, as you read this, close your eyes and imagine that ALL is forgiven, including the past and current worrisome issues. The power to change your mind about what to think or how to think about it is up to you. This is where your true power lies. We have been brainwashed by parents, society, and governments and have accepted a set of beliefs, but we still have the choice to drop old judgments or hang on. Forgive and forget? You decide what to believe

We live in a dualistic world: good and bad, hot and cold, young and old, etc. We also have a split mind with two thought systems. We can listen to the ego, the voice of judgment and division, or the voice of Love and inclusion. YOU, the Decision Maker, decide which voice to follow. Choose the Holy Spirit (Love, Spirit, Source, God, Allah, Yahweh, Creator) and dwell in peace, or choose the ego's voice of judgment, guilt, and envy and dwell in fear. Watch your mind to see the thoughts you are choosing. If you feel stressed, you are choosing the ego's fear, pain, guilt, and hate. If you feel at peace, you are choosing equality, compassion, non-judgment, and kindness. You can tell which mind you are listening to by honestly asking: How do I feel? A forgiveness thought brings a soothing balm. A blaming, judgmental thought brings guilt and fear of attack. The ego thought system is designed to keep the misery, disharmony, guilt, and attack going. It can also make you sick, literally!

The purpose of the world is to learn the lesson of forgiveness. Forgiveness is our function as we live our lives: marriage, partnership, career, family, etc. When you are upset, there is something to forgive. We can be hurt by nothing but our thoughts, and we can change all thoughts that hurt. For example: Someone at work really bothers you; he/she is a loudmouth, controlling, back-stabbing, conniving busybody. Ask the voice for Love/ Spirit in your mind: How can I see this differently? Then wait. A thought will come, maybe in the next few minutes, hour, or later, but hang tight! Keep asking. The answer will be quiet and calm. It will bring a feeling of release and peace. It is the Holy Spirit, the voice for love within your mind. Conversely, the ego voice will have more judgments and blame.

When we see a person or situation differently, we understand that it was just a mistake. Perhaps we end up looking at our perceptions, expectations, and/or projections. A projection is a judgment that we project out, onto someone else in order not to recognize it in ourselves. Like disliking someone who constantly interrupts when we in fact do the same thing but no one tells us!

How freeing to have a mind at rest! When tenseness, headache, or worry sets in, there is something to forgive. Forgive, release, and laugh at it! Remember, your true identity is Spirit, eternal, residing in Oneness and Loved. How can the eternal be hurt? Choose the decision-making mind, and listen to Spirit, the eternal that is in you. Forgiveness enters and heals all wounds, judgments, and grievances. We all have had painful experiences that seem beyond the forgiveness factor. The question is: How long do you want to hold onto the pain? We have a high tolerance for pain. It will last as long as you withhold forgiveness. Be pain-free and forgive the world and everyone for everything!

> "In many only the spark remains, for the Great Rays are
> obscured. Yet God has kept the spark alive so that the
> Rays can never be completely forgotten. If you but see
> the little spark you will learn of the greater light, for
> the Rays are there unseen. Perceiving the spark will
> heal, but knowing the light will create."
> A Course In Miracles T -10.IV.8:1-4

VALENTINE'S DAY: WHY NOT LOVE YOURSELF?

Ask a friend to read the following paragraph to you as you close your eyes and relax. Then, do the same for them:

"You are the light of the World. You are complete and healed and whole. You are loved, loving, and lovable. The beauty and grandeur of your true identity is sung to by the angels. The happiness of heaven surrounds you now and into eternity where loneliness does not exist. The Universe looks to you for completion. The realization of your true identity as Spirit brings its healing light to any regrets, self-judgments, and concerns. Exclude no one, including yourself, from your light. Picture yourself surrounded in a glowing sphere of light. Invite everyone to join you. Remind yourself daily of your light, your identity, by saying: I am the light of the world. I extend love to all whom I meet. Namaste."

You can change your thoughts about yourself. The question is: Do you want to? Just because you believe something does not mean it is true. We all have made mistakes, have millions of regrets, wonder why we didn't do something we think we should have, or why we didn't listen, and the list goes on and on. Has this type of thinking made you happier? When you are in a hole, stop digging. Forgiveness is the answer, but I don't mean getting down on your knees and begging. Just forgive because you are Spirit having a human experience and residing in a body, in a classroom called the World. People are not perfect. Everyone has made mistakes. But spirit is Perfection and has done nothing wrong. You are not who you think you are.

When we give, we also receive. Extend the Love within your mind to everyone and every living thing—your family, friends, enemies, and associates—but make sure to leave no one out. When you are kind, your journey and the classroom will be peaceful and joyful. Love is eternal and unceasing, and it cannot run out. You can give away all the love you want. It will never run out. It is like the magic pot of pudding in the children's story that boils over unceasingly. Except, love does not make a mess of things, rather it cleans things up. It is a mind-training practice to remember the limitless love within. Holding it in your mind, it is yours.

At some level you know Spirit, not ego, is your true identity. Numerous daily repetitions will set the belief in your mind. The ego thoughts in your mind will resist. In fact, ego will probably tell you the opposite and deny the reality of what you are. To learn more about how the ego works, I suggest Eckhart Tolle's book, A New Earth, Awakening to Your Life's Purpose, and in particular, chapter two on the ego.

When you feel upset, remember to connect to the unconditional, non-judgmental light within. You do not have to believe in God. Just believe in love. You have the power to extend it to yourself, to others and the world. Many spiritual traditions tell us love is God or God is love. Think of it this way: Whenever you have a loving thought, you are an extension of love whether you call it God/Creator/Yahweh/Great Spirit/Allah, and you are the creator of how you perceive your life and your world. You are light, and it is always accessible no matter what is going on in your life. Exclude no one from your love, including yourself.

> *"Listen,—perhaps you catch a hint of an ancient*
> *state not quite forgotten; dim, perhaps, and yet not*
> *altogether unfamiliar, like a song whose name is*
> *long forgotten, and the circumstances in which you*
> *heard completely unremembered. Not the whole song*
> *has stayed with you, but just a little wisp of melody,*
> *attached not to a person or a place or anything*
> *particular. But you remember, from just this little part*
> *how lovely was the song, how wonderful the setting*
> *where you heard it, and how you loved those who*
> *were there and listened with you."*
> A Course In Miracles T-21.I.6:1-3

KNOW YOUR TRUE IDENTITY: WHO ARE YOU?

A good friend of mine died recently. She had gone through a year of cancer treatment. When she first became sick and the terrible word "cancer" was mentioned by her doctor, and since we were on similar spiritual paths, I gently reminded her that her true identity was Spirit and that she was not her body. "I know that!" she said emphatically! Everyone who knew her—doctors, radiologists, friends and family were shown by the guidance of her Great Spirit that she was indeed not her body. Yes, her body was losing hair and weight, and yes, it was not very hungry, but she did not identify with it as being her identity. She knew her identity was her higher Spirit Self, one with her Creator, loved, loving, and lovable.

What seems to keep us from us from inner peace is very simply not realizing or accepting our true identity. We are born into a body, so we totally identify with it as being who we are, but many religions and spiritualties tell us otherwise. We are told that our true reality over and above is body is Spirit. Your Spirit is eternal. It is ageless, formless, can never die and, being invulnerable, cannot be threatened. That truth, if accepted, brings peace to a frantic mind. The process is to let go of the ego identity and the thoughts that try to convince us that the body is everything that we are. That it has certain needs, with a particular DNA, and is subject to germs, illnesses, has a particular birth identity, and belongs to a certain ethnic group. There are thousands of forms of separation in the world, but we all have the same identity beyond the body that makes us the same—i.e., Spirit.

But what happens when the body dies? It is gently laid down, thanked for its usefulness, and our Spirit continues. Love was who my friend was regardless of the condition of her body. I know she had some struggles, but since her spiritual path was one of not believing in the reality of death and she had trained her mind well, the problems were solved. She gave Love in the silence or kindness she offered. She never met a "stranger." If you happen to recall meeting a perky lady with a colorful hat, sharing a statement of hope or encouragement, that was her. She never excluded anyone from her Love, just like God! She had a large collection of hats matching the outfit of the day that she perched in a cocky manner on her bald head. Sometimes she took the hat off just to show that, after all, she was more than her body image or her ego.

The time came when she had to wear an oxygen tube in her nose. Would that stop her? She went everywhere, pulling the metal oxygen canister behind her, and sang at Rogue Valley Peace Choir performances. She always asked for help when she needed to maneuver the canister. Many probably thought, "Why doesn't she just stay home and take it easy?" But she was not going to let a little thing like a metal canister or a body with cancer stop her from expressing joy and Love. She was teaching those lucky enough to know her that she did not identify with the body. She had a sick body, but it was not everything she was! She finally left her body, leaving it on the bed like a shell or a chrysalis, and with grace and a peace that is not of this world, her Spirit exited the illusion. What is the point of death anyway? It is a mystery. However, we know the body is a means for communication; we care for it as an aid in negotiating the classroom of life and learning our lessons, but it is not everything we are. My friend did not slink away to hide the body in the dying process. She taught us that it was not who she was, and neither are we. Maybe inner peace is getting to know our identity is Spirit, always free to forgive, love, and let go.

> *"Miracles reawaken the awareness that the spirit,*
> *not the body, is the altar of truth. This is the recognition*
> *that leads to the healing power of the miracle."*
> A Course In Miracles T - 1. Miracle 20.

DON'T BLAME GOD!

Do you often wonder where the term "Act of God" came from? It probably originated in ancient times when the gods were believed to be responsible for everything unexplainable. It put some "order" on chaos in order to explain the inexplicable. When disaster struck, such as a tsunami, earthquake, hurricane, horrible accident, disease, or death, there was no reasonable explanation, so God took the hit. Some research tells me it is a legal term coined in the 1800's for events out of human control for which no person can be held responsible. But why blame God for the misery of the world? Psychologically, we very neatly do what Sigmund Freud defined as projection: something we cannot accept we project onto someone else. That is what we do to God or anyone we blame for unrest. Throughout the ages, we have collectively projected our dark side onto others and especially onto God, because we cannot tolerate it within. We deceive ourselves into thinking the problem is with someone else rather than within ourselves. Poor old God takes the hit.

We have free will so that we can make choices; however, many are miserable and bereft of comfort for having thrown comfort away. Like the baby, God went out with the bath water. Projecting "hateful old man" on God is an act of fear. We think he is out to get us with his lightning bolt. Ask yourself if blaming God for the world's misery is worth throwing love away. God cannot represent both love and fear. That is like mixing oil and water. God is one or the other. God does not control your life or your thinking—you do. What you think is up to you. Give up blaming chaos on God, or you will deprive yourself of Love. Remember your thoughts are not always true.

If God is LOVE, as many spiritual traditions believe the Creator to be, then surely such energy could never create evil or malice. A Loving God would never create wars, torture, havoc, birth defects, disease, death, or natural disasters.

Speaking of natural disasters, insurance companies need to stop using the term "an act of God" in their policies. Scientists tell us that global warming is the cause for more intense hurricanes, stronger storms, and the shift in world weather patterns. Did God create global warming? Nope. You and I did, and still do.

There is no doubt that God is a great mystery. If there are a zillion people on the planet, there will be a zillion different concepts of what this mystery might be. But for the time being, let's stop calling disasters Acts of God and quit blaming God for misery on earth. Let's rid ourselves of the worn-out concept that God is an invisible being, bent on our destruction. That concept has been engrained into our thinking by our ego—not God's.

When you enter the beautiful solid glass doors at SOU's Schneider Museum of Art, Ashland, OR look down and you will see these words engraved on a large granite stone: "Art is a Gift from God."

If Art is a gift, then through our gift of creativity we find evidence of God. Everyone is creative! What do we do with gifts? We share them. We sing, dance, paint, draw, drum, count; we create music, songs, symphonies; we write books and poetry; we design buildings, bridges and E=mc2...all gifts to be shared with the world.

Creativity also includes the aspects of compassion, trust, tolerance, generosity, faithfulness, gentleness, patience, kindness, goodness, and more. Next time you think "Act of God," visit a museum or create something, and remember God is in the business of Love; so do something you Love, and you will be closer to God! An Act of God is something that comes from love flowing through you and into the world. You are acting on behalf of love.

"I rest in God." This thought will bring to you the rest and quiet, peace and stillness, and the safety and the happiness you seek. "I rest in God." This thought has power to wake the sleeping truth in you, whose vision sees beyond appearances to that same truth in everyone and everything there is. Here is the end of suffering for all the world, and everyone who ever came and yet will come to linger for a while."
A Course In Miracles W-109.2:1-5

Sally J. McKirgan

Walking on Water!

What a wonderful dream that came to me last night!
I love the possibilities this dream brings to light.
We all have incredible fanciful nightly dreams
May one like this soon visit your minds holy screen:
An old woman was frantic to cross the river.
Bridges were left and right, too far off to please her.
Since I could walk on water I offered to assist.
She was ready to go, with no thought to resist.
We walked upon the water, towards the distant shore,
Crossing the dark flowing river her faith was restored.
A doubt crept into my mind that her cane would stick,
into the water; we'd fall in and get soaking wet.
Because the doubting thought and the entrance of fear
it happened! Just like that! So fears come true my dear.
Knowing it was easy, on water to walk about,
I climbed up on top again and pulled her right out.
Our walk resumed and safely at shore we arrived.
I bid her goodbye, then met friends in a wood nearby.
I ponder the meaning from this wondrous dream:
All is possible but don't listen to doubt it seems.
Always avoid the fears, remember what you can do.
By recalling your options, nothing's too hard for you.
Now I feel empowered and limitless day or night,
Because God knows it's across the water I walk at night.

Painting Watercolor: Title Walking on Water by Sally
McKirgan – prints available: sally-mckirgan.pixels.com

THE GIFT OF THE GREAT RAYS

THE GIFT OF THE GREAT RAYS

When experience will come to end your doubting has been set. W-158.4

This most inexplicable beautiful mystical experience happened Christmas 1987. Earlier that year, in April I discovered the Course and began in the workbook with its 365 lessons, one for each day of the year. I was drawn to the Workbook because the Text looked daunting to me but I attended a study group at the Walnut Creek Unity where the text was the focus. I committed to doing a lesson per day no matter if I "got it" or not.

That Christmas I was working in downtown San Francisco at my husband's company and often ran banking errands. I would always read the daily lesson in the morning and then repeat it throughout the day and particularly as I walked about the City. San Francisco was decked out, as usual, with Holiday decorations and amonst the throngs of shoppers it was chaotic and exciting. The weather was cold and a damp December fog hung in the air. That day walking back to the office, I was on O'Farrell Street, across from Macy's, waiting for the light to change. I noticed a group of homeless people sitting in front of Macy's Christmas window, and in particular a young woman, sitting on a blanket holding a baby in her lap. The thought went through my mind: "That could be Mary and Jesus sitting on that hard street, cold and hungry and no warm mangers to be found in San Francisco." I reached into my purse and pulled out a dollar to give to her as I walked by. The light turned green and I proceeded across the street. Her hair was long golden reddish curly and her face pale and slightly freckled. The baby was in her lap, wrapped in a blue blanket. Her head was bent forward and she was writing a sign with her free hand asking for money for help. I learned down and giving her my dollar I said "God Bless." She looked up and said "Thank You" in one of the warmest voices I have ever heard.

That's when our eyes locked. The gift I gave was puny and insignificant in comparison to what she gave me. Her gift was the sight of Great Heavenly Rays! As I looked down into her eyes, I saw Great Rays of light shooting heavenward, up to the right. It was as if I didn't have a head or a body because I was leaning over looking down at her, but I saw the Rays going up! I was so shocked I stepped back immediately, eyes brimming with tears I stumbled up the street. As I walked back I was numb! All I could think was "what on earth happened?" When I got to the office I opened my mouth to tell my husband, but either the phone rang or he started to speak. He was so busy he didn't notice my bewilderment. I thought maybe I should go back and see her but actually felt afraid! Words cannot do justice to this profound mystical experience and every time I tell the story the tears come. I wrote a poem which helped me process the experience. I even sent a letter to editor of the S.F. Examiner and copied Macy's but they must have had a good laughed. Months later I mentioned it to a few Course friends but my words fell on bewildered ears and the tears always came. I have had several psychic experiences but this was by far the most consequential for my life and profoundly earth-shattering. It is always with me to soften extreme upsets, the grief of a son's early death and that of my husband. This mystery proves to me "God Is" there is no death because I know there is a Reality beyond what our eyes see or ears hear.

Remarkably, this experience happened before I knew that the Great Rays were mentioned in the Course several times and once in the Workbook.

Looking back, I believe that on the day of the encounter, I was likely on Lesson 245 since I started the Course in mid-April. Lesson 245 – Your Peace is with me, Father, I am safe.

1. *"Your peace is with me, Father I am safe. Where I go, Your peace goes there with me. It sheds its light on everyone I meet. I bring it to the desolate and lonely and afraid. I give Your peace to those who suffer pain, or grieve for loss, or think they are bereft of hope and happiness. Send them to me Father. Let me bring your peace with me. For I would save Your Son, as is Your Will, that I may come to recognize my Self."*

2. *And so we go in peace. To all the world we give the message that we have received. And thus we come to hear the Voice for God, Who speaks to us as we relate His Word; Whose Love we recognize because we share the World that He has given unto us.*
A Course In Miracles W-pll - 245

It is called a Holy Instant, a Revelation perhaps but it convinced me there is a Reality beyond this worldly plane and although I struggle at times, I know the Course is True. I have sometimes doubted I could accomplish it but then again, what choice do I have when I know the Love in its pages isTrue and I want the Peace of God above all else.

Sally J. McKirgan

The Gift of The Great Rays

It happened one Christmas Season, in front of Macy's store.
There she sat on O'Farrell Street, holding her baby near the door.
On a thin blanket with brightly, decorated windows behind,
Her sweet blue bundle in her arms, the cold fog soon to entwine.
And writing a sign with one hand, asking for money for help
Shoppers busily passed them by with eyes and hearts unfelt.
Because at Merry Christmas time, we are in such a crazy rush,
We do not want to see the pain, and so our minds say "hush."
But when I saw her lovely face and blond red hair aflame
My only thought: "Mary and Jesus! That could be their names!"
Taking one dollar from my purse I hastened across the street.
And kneeling I said "God Bless" that's when our eyes did meet.
What happened next mystifies me; warmly she said "Thank You"
I fought back tears I did not know exactly where to turn to.
The gifts she gave: Brilliant Rays, ascending to Heavenly Love.
Silent Rays, rising right and reaching The Magnificence Above.
It was as if a choir of Angels had gathered nearby on wing
To glorify all life and Bach's Mass in B Minor to sing.
Many times I've tried to explain the vision from her blue eyes.
But words seem inadequate and how can LOVE be described?
How could that puny dollar have deserved such a priceless gift?
I was speechless and could hardly think; it left my heart bereft.
The gift of grace she gave to me far grander than mine to her.
God above forever help me be grateful for love so pure.
You may not believe this miracle in front of Macy's store,
It's been said to give and receive are what Holidays are for.
But if you will believe and recall come this Christmas Season.
That when you give; you too receive and God's Love is the Reason!

Painting Watercolor: Title Angel Star – All watercolor
prints available: sally-mckirgan.pixels.com

THE PROMISE OF THE GREAT RAYS

In the Course there are seven references to the term "Great Rays." Here are the quotes and where they are in the Course including one in the Manual's Clarification of Terms Epilogue that mentions the word Ray.

Chapter 10.

1. In many only the spark remains, for the Great Rays are obscured. Yet God has kept the spark alive so that the Rays can never be completely forgotten. If you but see the little spark you will learn of the greater light, for the Rays are there unseen. T-10.IV.8:1-3

Chapter 15.

2. As the ego would limit your perception of your brothers to the body, so would the Holy Spirit release your vision and let you see the Great Rays shining from them, so unlimited that they reach to God. It is this shift to vision that is accomplished in the holy instant. T-15.IX.1:1-2

3. In the holy instant, where the Great Rays replace the body in awareness, the recognition of relationships without limits is given you. But in order to see this, it is necessary to give up every use the ego has for the body, and to accept the fact that the ego has no purpose you would share with it. T-15.IX.3:1-2

Chapter 16.

4. The Great Rays would establish the total lack of value of the special relationship, if they were seen. For in seeing them the body would disappear, because its value would be lost. T-16.VI.4:5-6)

5. Across the bridge it is so different. For a time the body is still seen, but not exclusively, as it is seen here. The little spark that holds the Great Rays within it is also visible, and this spark cannot be limited long to littleness. Once you have crossed the bridge, the value of the body is so

diminished in your sight that you will see no need at all to magnify it. T-16.VI.6:1-4

Chapter 18.

6. You have found your brother, and you will light each other's way. And from this light will the Great Rays extend back into darkness and forward unto God, to shine away the past and so make room for His eternal Presence, in which everything is radiant in the light. T-18. III.8:6-7

Workbook Lesson pII 360.

Father, it is Your peace that I would give, receiving it of You. I am Your Son, forever just as You created me, for the Great Rays remain forever still and undisturbed within me. I would reach to them in silence and in certainty, for nowhere else can certainty be found. Peace be to me, and peace to all the world. In holiness were we created, and in holiness do we remain. Your Son is like to You in perfect sinlessness. And with this thought we gladly say "Amen." W-360.1:1-7)

The Clarification of Terms Epilogue

You are a stranger here. But you belong to Him Who loves you as He loves Himself. Ask but my help to roll the stone away, and it is done according to His Will. We have begun the journey. Long ago the end was written in the stars and set into the Heavens with a shining Ray that held it safe within eternity and through all time as well. And holds it still; unchanged, unchanging and unchangeable. C-ep.2:1-6

> *"And so we offer blessing to all things, uniting lovingly with all the world, which our forgiveness has made one with us."*
> A Course In Miracles, W p11 – 283.2

ABOUT: A COURSE IN MIRACLES

The Course was published in 1973. It has a 669 page text; a workbook with 365 lessons for each day of the year that help re-train the mind; The Manual for Teachers; Clarification of Terms and two additional pamphlets; Psychotherapy Purpose and Practice and the Song of Prayer.

The Course is metaphysical, psychological with Christian, Eastern, Freudian, and Platonic themes of enduring Truth intertwined in its non-dual spiritual scope. It came from the Love in the Mind of Jesus to the scribe, Helen Schucman, a psychologist at the Columbia Presbyterian Medical Center in New York City in 1965. As the assistant to Dr. William Thetford, it came in answer to their call to "find a better way" to work and live in the world. You may find it hard to believe the source as Jesus, but as you read the quotes that are interspersed, remember that they come from a loving source that is to me, unlike any other found in this world. The complete amazing history can be found at the website of The Foundation for Inner Peace www.acim.org

In the text, workbook and manual for teachers, Jesus guides us to the home we never left. He tells us he is our equal and elder brother, a Son of God, yes, along with each one of us. What he accomplished however still is our potential and the Course will help us accomplish just that. He defines sin as "lack of love" a mistake to be corrected and he gently helps us to look at and correct our perceptions, judgments and undo the blocks to the awareness of love's presence in our Mind. He helps us understand the ego, the false mind that we listened to at the time of separation from God, which never really happened because it is impossible to be separate from our Source. That Source is in our Mind whether we acknowledge That Fact or not, but we need help to find our way out of the dream, the illusion. We suffer believing that sin, guilt and fear are real. We are told we are the light of the world and it is the Christ Self in us that seeks to awaken to Truth and end suffering.

This is a self-study Course with teachers all over the world. Jesus tells us that if a teacher is needed, it will happen. In Workbook Lesson 70 "*If it helps you, think of me holding your hand and leading you. And I assure you this will be no idle fantasy.* W-70.9:3-41

AFTERWORD

The longing for inner peace is what led me to discover A Course In Miracles and the ultimate mystical and profound experience of the Great Rays. I am not special because of the experience. I am like you and we are part of everything, we are the same. Many, perhaps you as well, have had experiences yet may not reveal them for fear of being judged. We hide them like we hide from God but they are His gifts! Sometimes Course students believe years of study are needed however; I'm proof that's untrue.

Jesus explains: "*When the ego was made, God placed in the mind the Call to joy. This Call is so strong that the ego always dissolves at Its sound. That is why you must choose to hear one of two voices within you.* T-5.II.3:2.3

The ego's world is primarily chaos with a little beauty thrown in, and earlier I wondered if God really created it. The Course says he didn't. The Course leads us gently in undoing the ego allowing the love to flow and gradually dissolve the blocks within the mind. Free from the ego, we see that everything is either love or a call for love. That is the challenge and the promise of the Course: to recognize that Love that is our natural inheritance.

The Course promises inner peace but we hold the key to that promise. We can choose peace this second but only when we want it and ask the Holy Spirit or Jesus for help to see differently. Don't ask the ego. Only the voice for God, the Holy Spirit within, can help us see through the darkness and to the door that is always open. It may sound like magic but love was placed in the mind as our inheritance. That Love will offer the answer to any question. Be calm, ask the Holy Spirit and wait and listen and don't judge. Darkness is always dissolved by light. Love is available; reach for it within your Holy Mind and be free!

The Great Rays, the Greatest Gift are in you, everyone, every living thing. Embrace them and Welcome the power of Holy Love that emanates to you forever; from the Heart of God and back.

RESOURCES & RECOMMENDATIONS AND READINGS

Foundation for Inner Peace – Publisher of the Course in 27 languages. P.O. Box 598 Mill Valley, CA 94942 www.acim.org The entire Course can be read online and the lessons can be listened to. They offer webinars, blogs and discussions online.

Foundation for A Course In Miracles. Founder Dr. Kenneth Wapnick 375 N. Stephanie Street, Suite 2311, Henderson, NV 89014 www.facim. org Dedicated to the teachings of Dr. Kenneth Wapnick through his many books, recordings, DVD and weekly live streaming classes. Dr. Wapnick wrote Absence from Felicity, the story of Helen Schucman and her scribing of A Course In Miracles.

Miracle Distribution Center 3947 E. La Palma Avenue, Anaheim, CA 92807. www.miraclecenter.org The center publishes a monthly newsletter, has weekly livestream lessons on line and a source of books and miracles classes held all over the world.

A School for A Course In Miracles, Denver, CO founded by Lyn Corona and Tim Wise in 2007 under "The Ark of Peace" dedicated to honoring Jesus' devoted helper and their friend and teacher, Dr. Kenneth Wapnick whose illumination of the Course is unparalleled in depth and breadth. www.schoolforacourseinmiracles.org They offer weekly classes and class replays on the youtube channel.

Pathways of Light - Rev Myron Jones is a Pathways of Light minister. Rev Jones is the author of Hey, Holy Spirit, It's Me Again. www. forgivenessisthewayhome.org

Bonnie L. Greenwell, PHD, Title "When Spirit Leaps, Navigating the Process of Spiritual Awakening." This book is helpful in explaining the various mystical experiences for those who need to understand them.

Adyashanti – Resurrecting Jesus: Embodying the Spirit of a Revolutionary Genius

REFERENCES

vii (https://acim.org/acim/en/s/785#1:1-7 | W-360.1:1-7) Paragraph 1
vii (https://acim.org/acim/en/s/510#4:5-7 | W-106.4:5-7) Paragraph 2
Page 3 (https://acim.org/acim/en/s/289#6:5-6 | T-25.V.6:5-6)
Page 5 (https://acim.org/acim/en/s/198#1:1-4 | T-15.IX.1:1-4)
Page 7 (https://acim.org/acim/en/s/76#3:1-3 | T-3.VI.3:1-3)
Page 8 (https://acim.org/acim/en/s/207#6:1-3 | T-16.VI.6:1-3)
Page 27 (https://acim.org/acim/en/s/205#2:1-2 | T-16.IV.2:1-2)
Page 29 (https://acim.org/acim/en/s/90#7:8-10 | T-5.II.7:8-10)
Page 31 (https://acim.org/acim/en/s/471#6:3 | W-68.6:3)
Page 32 (https://acim.org/acim/en/s/267#15:1 | T-22.VI.15:1)
Page 41 (https://acim.org/acim/en/s/938#10:5-7 | S-3.IV.10:5-7)
Page 47 (https://acim.org/acim/en/s/200#2:1-2 | T-15.XI.2:1-2)
Page 48 (https://acim.org/acim/en/s/54#3:3-13 | T-1.II.3:3-13)
Page 48 (https://acim.org/acim/en/s/270#1:1-2 | T-23.I.1:1-2)
Page 48 (https://acim.org/acim/en/s/309#1:1-2 | T-27.IV.1:1-2)
Page 48 (https://acim.org/acim/en/s/190#1:1 | T-15.I.1:1)
Page 56 (https://acim.org/acim/en/s/221#8:1-7 | T-18.III.8:1-7)
Page 63 (https://acim.org/acim/en/s/142#8:1-3 | T-10.IV.8:1-3)
Page 72 (https://acim.org/acim/en/s/221#1:4-8 | T-18.III.1:4-8)
Page 75 (https://acim.org/acim/en/s/485#1:2-5 | W-81.1:2-5)
Page 78 (https://acim.org/acim/en/s/233#6:1-10 | T-19.IV-A.6:1-10)
Page 84 (https://acim.org/acim/en/s/529#2:1-3 | W-124.2:1-3)
Page 90 (https://acim.org/acim/en/s/632#4:1-3 | W-pII.1.4:1-3)
Page 94 (https://acim.org/acim/en/s/460#1:1-9 | W-57.1:1-9)
Page 100 (https://acim.org/acim/en/s/57#1:5-8 | T-1.V.1:5-8)
Page 104 (https://acim.org/acim/en/s/699#1:5-7 | W-281.1:5-7)
Page 110 (https://acim.org/acim/en/s/88#3:5-8 | T-5.in.3:5-8)
Page 118 (https://acim.org/acim/en/s/573#1:5-7 | W-167.1:5-7)
Page 120 (https://acim.org/acim/en/s/858#2:4-6 | C-ep.2:4-6)
Page 122 (https://acim.org/acim/en/s/562#4:1-4 | W-156.4:1-4)
Page 126 (https://acim.org/acim/en/s/198#1:1 | T-15.IX.1:1)
Page 134 (https://acim.org/acim/en/s/488#3:2-6 | W-84.3:2-6)

Page 136 (https://acim.org/acim/en/s/270#1:1-2 | T-23.I.1:1-2)
Page 141 (https://acim.org/acim/en/s/145#3:5-10 | T-11.in.3:5-10)
Page 144 (https://acim.org/acim/en/s/938#4:1-6 | S-3.IV.4:1-6)
Page 146 (https://acim.org/acim/en/s/187#11:4-6 | T-14.X.11:4-6)
Page 150 (https://acim.org/acim/en/s/312#15:3-4 | T-27.VII.15:3-4)
Page 157 (https://acim.org/acim/en/s/149#6:3-5 | T-11.IV.6:3-5)
Page 160 (https://acim.org/acim/en/s/92#8:2-6 | T-5.IV.8:2-6)
Page 168 (https://acim.org/acim/en/s/704#1:1-9 | W-286.1:1-9)
Page 174 (https://acim.org/acim/en/s/656#1:1-5 | W-242.1:1-5)
Page 177 (https://acim.org/acim/en/s/200#8:1-3 | T-15.XI.8:1-3)
Page 182 (https://acim.org/acim/en/s/142#8:1-4 | T-10.IV.8:1-4)
Page 184 (https://acim.org/acim/en/s/252#6:1-3 | T-21.I.6:1-3)
Page186 (https://acim.org/acim/en/s/53#20:1-2 | T-1.I.20:1-2)
Page 189 (https://acim.org/acim/en/s/513#2:1-5 | W-109.2:1-5)
Page 196 (https://acim.org/acim/en/s/659#1:1-2:3 | W-245.1:1–2:3)
Page 201 (https://acim.org/acim/en/s/142#8:1-4 | T-10.IV.8:1-4) Paragraph 1
Page 201 (https://acim.org/acim/en/s/198#1:1-2 | T-15.IX.1:1-2) Paragraph 2
Page 201 (https://acim.org/acim/en/s/198#3:1-2 | T-15.IX.3:1-2) Paragraph 3
Page 201 (https://acim.org/acim/en/s/207#4:5-6 | T-16.VI.4:5-6) Paragraph 4
Page 201 (https://acim.org/acim/en/s/207#6:1-4 | T-16.VI.6:1-4) Paragraph 5
Page 202 (https://acim.org/acim/en/s/221#8:6-7 | T-18.III.8:6-7) Paragraph 1
Page 202 (https://acim.org/acim/en/s/785#1:1-3 | W-360.1:1-3) Paragraph 2
Page 202 (https://acim.org/acim/en/s/858#2:1-6 | C-ep.2:1-6) Paragraph 3
Page 202 (https://acim.org/acim/en/s/701#2:2 | W-283.2:2)
Page 205 (https://acim.org/acim/en/s/90#3:2-6 | T-5.II.3:2-6)
Page 210 (https://acim.org/acim/en/s/80#8:5-7 | T-4.I.8:5-7)

BIO – SALLY J. (HAMMER WENSKY) MCKIRGAN

Artist, poet and founder, editor of the inner peace column published weekly in the Ashland Daily Tidings, Ashland, OR, January 2009 to October 2022. She discovered A Course In Miracles over 35 years ago, attended, lectures, workshops, classes and currently facilitates a study group.

She held various positions in the Non-profit field from administrator, manager to fundraiser for Shelter, Inc. Concord, CA; The Shelter for Abused Women and The Conservancy of SW Florida both in Naples, FL.

Her lifelong desire to be an artist led her to study at the University of Washington and the Academy of Art, San Francisco. She studied painting with Jade Fon, Charlotte Britton, George Post, Gerald Brommer and Miles Batt. Her painting "Eland" was included in the book "The Artist's Design" by Marie MacDonnell Roberts. She is a former member of San Francisco Women Artists, East Bay Watercolor Society and Oakland Art Association. She had one woman shows in San Francisco, CA., and Naples Florida. Her paintings are in private collections in the United States and the Soviet Union. All paintings in this book can be viewed in color at the Fine Art America website https://Sally-McKirgan.pixels.com under the collection heading: "Book - The Gift of the Great Rays."

As a student of A Course In Miracles, the Course has influenced her artistic vision with concepts of world peace and the shared identity of the One Self. Her painting "One Family, One Planet, One People" incorporates symbols of the world's many faiths that have arisen from the Source of LOVE they share And her painting, "Three Major Religions" places their symbols hanging together in space peacefully as

Christmas Ornaments. Her blog contains articles on living and studying the Course: www.innerpeaceforyou.com

Her study of the course inspired writing and journaling and consequently led to sending the letter to the editor in 2008 that began the Ashland Tidings inner peace column.

She currently lives in Olympia, WA and tries to avoid getting into trouble.

"You are part of reality, which stands unchanged beyond the reach of your ego but within easy reach of spirit. When you are afraid, be still and know that God is real, and that you are His Beloved Son in whom He is well pleased. Do not let your ego dispute this, because the ego cannot know what is as far beyond its reach as you are."
A Course in Miracles T-4.8:5-7

Printed in the United States
by Baker & Taylor Publisher Services